Thomas Finlayson Henderson

Old-World Scotland

Glimpses of its Modes and Manners

Thomas Finlayson Henderson

Old-World Scotland
Glimpses of its Modes and Manners

ISBN/EAN: 9783744729925

Printed in Europe, USA, Canada, Australia, Japan

Cover: Foto ©ninafisch / pixelio.de

More available books at **www.hansebooks.com**

OLD-WORLD
SCOTLAND

Glimpses of its Modes and Manners

BY

T. F. HENDERSON

London

T. FISHER UNWIN

PATERNOSTER SQUARE

MDCCCXCIII

NOTE

The Author begs to acknowledge his obligations to the proprietors of the *National Observer* for their kind and ready courtesy in permitting the republication of the papers in this volume originally contributed to that journal.

The paper on "Kirk Discipline" has been widened in scope; to others additions have been made; and that on "New Light on the Darnley Murder" is printed for the first time.

CONTENTS.

OLD-WORLD SCOTLAND.

I.

DE QUINCEY, who has some claims as an authority on intoxicants, has opined that our northern climates have universally the taste latent, if not developed, for powerful liquors. He may be right; but, as a matter of fact, the taste has developed very slowly. In early times it prevailed chiefly in climates where the grape was grown, or in latitudes where bang and similar brews fired the savage breast. Moreover, once a race has made choice of its liquor, it clings thereto with a more than superstitious tenacity, and may be induced to change even its

religion with less reluctance and a lighter
sense of misgiving. It seems ultimately to
be less a matter of appetite or gustation
than of sentiment. By its connection with
the rites of hospitality and the main epi-
sodes of social life the liquor of a people
becomes in some sort the symbol of its
patriotism and its nobler human feelings.
Doubtless the increase of travel, the inter-
mixture of races, and the intercommunion
between nations may tend partly to oblite-
rate such predilections; but now, as of old,
it will generally be found that, at least
in the case of intoxicants, the adoption,
even partially, by one nation of another's
liquor is to some extent an evidence of
reciprocal respect and goodwill. It was
not till after the accession of Dutch William
to the throne of England that Englishmen
began to develop that affection for gin
which in the beginning of the eighteenth
century led to such extraordinary excesses.
The English vogue for Scottish whisky
also has been at least coincident with a

better appreciation of the Scot. Possibly some of the more ardent of the Southron votaries of the liquor have a lurking suspicion that it has a not very remote connection with the Scot's persistency and "cannieness"; that while "the haillsome parritch" is perhaps in some degree responsible for his stamina, whisky even more than Calvinism has been his main discipline and inspiration. Historically, however, whisky is not more the national liquor of Scotland than the kilt is the national dress, or Gaelic the national language. The only difference is that, while the dress and language of the Highland Celt seem alike destined to disappear at no distant date, whisky has not only survived the conquest of the Highlands, but has extended its empire to the Lowlands as well.

Originally the national liquor of Lowland Scotland, as of "Merrie England," was ale, the universal liquor of the Saxons. There is abundant evidence that ale was the

universal beverage in the Lowlands as early
as the thirteenth century, and the presumption is that its use in Caledonia was
coeval with the arrival of our Saxon forefathers. True, among the nobles wine was
very much in use from the thirteenth
century onwards, and for several centuries
it was drunk among the upper classes more
generally in Scotland than in England.
The Scottish vogue for wine was greatly
owing to the friendly relations between
Scotland and France. The staple was
claret, though Malvoisie, Canary, Madeira,
and other wines were imported at an early
period. Still, claret never became the
Scots national liquor, and although occasionally sold by Edinburgh vintners at a
very early period it could not be had in
good country inns till the eighteenth century. In " The Friars of Berwick," which
may be assigned to the end of the fifteenth
or beginning of the sixteenth century, the
" silly friars," Robert and Allan, are regaled
" in the wonder good hostelrie " without the

town on "stoups of ale with bread and
cheese"; and there was evidently nothing
better on tap, for among the materials
brought by the amorous Friar John for his
surreptitious feast with the landlady, while
the other friars were supposed to be asleep
in the loft, were—

> " Ane pair of bossis * good and fine
> They hold ane gallon-full of Gascon wine."

That ale was at this period considered good
enough even for the richest merchants may
also be inferred from the "Priests of Peebles."
The successful trafficker therein described
had waxed

> " Sae full of worldis wealth and win
> His hand he wash in ane silver basin ";

but in regard to his table provisions it is
deemed sufficient to state that his wife
" had no doubt of dearth of *ale* nor bread."
In the regulations issued by the Scottish

* Earthen bottles.

Privy Council on August 27, 1602—about a century later—for the meals of the masters and bursars of the University of Glasgow ale is the only liquor recognised: "The first meis, consisting of the FYVE MAISTERIS, sall have to thair disjoyne * ane quhyte breid of ane pund wecht in a sowpe, with the remains of a peice beif or mutton resting of the former day, *with thair pynt of aill amangis thame.* To thair denner they sal have ordinarlie quhyt breid aneuch, *with fyve* choppnis of sufficient guid and better nor the common sell aill in the town, with ane dische of bruise, and ane uther of skink † or kaill, a piece of soddon muttoun, another of beif, salt or fresche, according to the season, ane roist of beif, salt or fresche, according to the season, ane roist of veill or muttoun with a foull or cunyng,‡ or a pair of dowis § or chikkins, or uther siclyk secund rost as the seasoun gevis. And siclyk to

* French *Déjeûner.*
† Strong soup without vegetables, resembling beef-tea.
‡ Rabbit.   § Pigeons.

thair supper." According to our modern notions, the solids on which the masters fared were more sumptuous than the liquids. The only meal at which liquor was allowed to the bursars was dinner: "ane quart of of aill." From the Acts passed by Parliament in the sixteenth century regulating the price of ale so that the seller might have no undue advantage of the buyer, it is plain that the liquor was regarded as a necessary article of diet. In those pre-Lawsonian years the design of the Acts was to encourage, not discourage, its use. Drunkenness does not appear to have been a popular vice. It was by no means severely dealt with even by the Reformers; and although after the Reformation regulations were passed in Edinburgh and other cities closing all taverns and alehouses at ten o'clock, this was a mere corollary of a regulation for clearing the streets at this hour; there was no intention to interfere with or limit the consumption of ale. In like manner an Act passed in 1605 reducing the number of ale-

houses on the borders was intended merely
to diminish the resorts of thieves and rievers.
Even the Covenanter Nicoll regarded the
placing, in 1659, of an additional impost on
ale by the town of Edinburgh as a positive
act of impiety, at which at the same instant
" God frae the heavens declared His anger
by sending thunder and unheard tempests
and storms."

The quantity of wine which about the
beginning of the sixteenth century came
into the general market appears to have
been comparatively small. In 1508 the
Edinburgh magistrates decided that the
vintners should appoint four or five persons
of their faculty to buy the " hule hoip " of
wine and divide it equally. For a long
while after, however, the king (or queen),
the prelates, and the nobility claimed wine
almost as a perquisite of their own. In the
reign of Mary Stuart regulations were more
than once passed, not only fixing its price
but forbidding the importers to sell their
supply until the " Queen, prelates, earls,

lords, and barons be first stakit"; and when
the wine duties were imposed in 1608 the
nobles were specially exempted from payment. It is curious, and perhaps edifying,
to note that John Knox, strongly as he
denounced the luxurious and sensuous
habits of the Catholic clergy of his time,
retained till his dying day that relish for
French wine which he had no doubt acquired when a priest. Much as he railed
against the French mote in Queen Mary's
eye, he was all unconscious of the beam of
French claret in his own. Amid the stern
and severe thoughts which seemed to form
the staple of his meditations on his death-
bed, as recorded by Richard Bannatyne, the
pleasant and kindly homeliness of the following incident stands out in curiously
piquant relief: "The Setterday," says
Bannatyne, "John Durie and Archibald
Stewart come in about twelve houris, not
knowing how seike he was; and for thair
cause come to the table, which was the last
tyme that ever he sat at ony thereafter; for

he caused pierce ane hoggeid of wine which was in the seller, and willed the said Archibald send for the same so long as it lasted, for he would never tarie [live] untill it were drunken."

Ultimately there were three varieties of Scots ale—small, household, and strong; but it is the household ale alone—the " tippenny " of the Act of Union, of Allan Ramsay and of Robert Burns—that is properly entitled to the name and dignity of the national liquor. Ale of a corresponding quality to that of Allsopp or Bass did not become a common beverage in Scotland till comparatively recent times. Until the union of the crowns there was practically no commercial intercourse between the two kingdoms. It was with the utmost difficulty that James VI., in 1599, could persuade Elizabeth's minister Cecil to grant the required license for the transportation to Holyrood of " twelve tuns of double London beer " (stout, no doubt) for the " King's dearest spouse," she, it was pathetically

pleaded, being "daily accustomed to drink of
the same"; but on his advent to the English
throne such restrictions were greatly modified. In 1610 an Act passed by the Privy
Council to regulate the price of English
beer in Scotland set forth that importers
should "sell each tun of the said beer for
£6, so that the retailer thereof may sell the
same for 18d. the pint, the penalty to be
£20 for each tun sold for more than £6."
Probably the design and result of such an
enactment was to greatly diminish the importation of English beer; at any rate the
Customs Act of 1663 had a very prejudicial
effect on this and other exports and manufactures. The question as to the duty to
be paid on Scots ale gave rise to considerable discussion in the debate on the Seventh
Article of Union. The one party held that
it should be taxed at the same rate as
English ale, the other at the same rate as
English small beer; but when the question
was examined in committee a medium duty
was agreed on. Subsequent changes in the

excise duties on malt led in Glasgow to
serious riots, and inspired the Jacobites with
delusive hopes of a successful rising.

Ale and claret are the liquors chiefly sung
by Allan Ramsay and by Robert Fergusson.
As every schoolboy does not know, honest
Allan immortalised two Edinburgh alewives
—Maggie Johnstoun, who kept the famous
golfers' house of call near Bruntsfield
Links—

> "Aften in Maggie's at hy-jinks *
>   We guzzled scuds,
>   Till we could scarce wi' halc-out drinks
>   Cast aff our duds."

and Lucky Wood in the Canongate, who

> "Ne'er gae in a lawin † fause,
>   Nor stoups a' froath aboon the hause,
>   Nor kept dowd tip ‡ within her waws,
>   But reaming swats ; §
>   She ne'er ran sour jute, because
>   It gies the batts." ‖

In Ramsay's day there was no such thing

---

* A drinking game.   † Reckoning.
‡ Stale tipple.   § New ale.   ‖ Colic.

as the modern "public." Ale, too, is the liquor quaffed in Fergusson's "Farmer's Ingle " :—

> "Weel kens the gudewife that the pleughs require
> A heartsome meltith, * an' refreshing synd †
> O' nappy ‡ liquor, o'er a bleezing fire :
> Sair wark an' pourtith § downa well be join'd.
> Wi' buttered bannocks now the girdle reeks :
> I' the far nook the bowie ‖ briskly reams."

In "Toddlin' Hame," which Burns thought "the first bottle song that ever was composed," nothing stronger than ale is mentioned :—

> "Fair fa' the gudewife, and send her gude sale !
> She gies us white bannocks to relish her ale ;
> Syne, if that her tippenny chance to be sma',
> We tak a guid scour o't and ca't awa'."

But, though Ramsay could be " blythe and fain " upon beer, he in certain moods indicates a special appreciation of claret,

---

* Meal.   † Draught.   ‡ Strong or good.
§ Poverty—scant fare.   ‖ Cask of beer.

especially in winter weather, when golf or
bowls were in abeyance :—

> " Then fling on coals, and ripe the ribs,
>   And beek * the house baith but and ben ;
> That mutchkin-stoup it huds but drips,
>   Then let's get *in the tappit hen.* †
> Good claret best keeps out the cauld,
>   And drives away the winter soon ;
> It makes a man baith gash ‡ and bauld,
>   And heaves his soul beyond the moon."

In the eighteenth century claret was
usually kept on tap in the best taverns.
Fergusson sings of one in Dumfries famed
for the liquor, and volunteers the opinion
that, if that " pleasant sinner " Q. H. F.
had been alive,

> " Nae mair he'd sing to auld Maecenas
>   The blinking een o' bonny Venus ;
> His leave at ance he wad hae ta'en us
>   For claret here."

---

* Warm—by means of a blazing fire.
† A bottle shaped like a hen, and holding three
quarts of claret.
‡ Wise.

Fergusson wrote some forty years later
than Ramsay. Occasionally he mentions
whisky and gin with approbation. It was
perhaps the introduction of these more
heady liquors that moved him to pen what
is probably the earliest extant teetotal ode,
his "Cauler Water," but his example in no
wise corresponded with its precept and sentiment.

Dr. Somerville in his "Own Life and
Times," referring to the period of his boy-
hood—about the middle of the eighteenth
century—thus writes: "In families of my
own rank the beverages offered to ordinary
visitors consisted of home-brewed ale and
of a glass of brandy; or, where there was
greater ceremony, claret and brandy punch."
For a time the importation of French wine
was stayed by the plague of Marseilles
(1720); but the use of claret, thus partially
interrupted in Scotland, was again resumed,
the real cause of its permanent decline as
the beverage of the Scottish middle and
upper classes being the outbreak of the

great war towards the close of the century. Port or other stronger wines were comparatively little drunk in the north till the present century. Thus, a cargo of port, brought by Sir Laurence Dundas in 1743, failed to find a ready sale; the Scottish palate was then unused to it, and it was necessity rather than preference that ultimately gave it its vogue.

The quality of our forefathers' liquor must be taken into consideration in determining the significance of such anecdotes as are illustrative of their convivial habits. Perhaps the comparative weakness of the tipple was responsible for their longer sittings. Vinous intoxication is also by no means so immediately hurtful as that produced by the stronger liquors, although possibly the taste "latent if not developed for powerful liquors" may have led to special excess in the use of the light wines. Otherwise the drinking customs of the better classes in Scotland were closely modelled on those of the French.

The tavern played quite as important a
part in the social life of Edinburgh as the
café continues still to do in the social life
of Paris or Marseilles. There the advo-
cate discussed his client's business over a
glass of claret or bottle of ale, and tavern
dinners were a common diversion even of
married men. In winter the wine was
mulled and drunk hot, sugar being used
with it before tea or coffee was popular.
But with the invasion of strong waters, the
respectability of the tavern departed.

In early times drinking in alehouses
was of the same prolonged character as
drinking in taverns, and for similar reasons.
Whisky is far too potent and speedy in
its effects for the old drinking game of
chance " high-jinks." " Scourging a nine-
gallon tree," which is, being interpreted,
drawing the spigot of a barrel of ale, and
never quitting it till it be drunk out, was
another roisterer's pastime; but (in spite
of Burns's witness to its merits), with a
staple of " tippenny " it must have been

alike comparatively innocuous and unspeak-
ably dreary. The excessive drinking indulged in at Lowland funerals in the
eighteenth century seems to have been
coincident with the transition from ale to
whisky. The provision of refreshments was
in many cases a necessity, on account of
the long distances some mourners had to
come. The ordinary was originally ale,
with bread and cheese ; but when whisky
began to be supplied on the same bounteous
scale as the milder beverage, the consequences were sometimes appallingly ludi-
crous and sometimes hideously indecent.

II.

WHAT about whisky during the centuries when ale and claret were the chief hand-maids to Scottish mirth? Had it no exis-tence? Were its virtues really unknown? Or did the Scot, in Burns's phrase, "twist" at it "his gruntle * wi' a glunch † o' sour disdain"? If it was unknown, who was its discoverer, or how was it introduced? At least a fairly satisfactory answer is pos-sible. So far as the bulk of the Lowlands is concerned, whisky was virtually non-existent as a beverage till near the close of the sixteenth century, and did not come into general use till very much later. The

* Snout. † Frown.

name of its creator does not survive even
in national myth; the circumstances atten-
dant upon its entrance on the stage of time
are involved in such a mystery as that
which shrouds the origin of species. The
probability is that the general benefactor
was some mighty "medicine man" of the
ancient Celts; but who he was and when
or where he first set up his still and called
spirits from the yeasty malt remains un-
recorded. It is, however, well-nigh in-
dubitable that in Scotland the original
manufacturers of whisky were the Celts
of the Highlands. Usquebagh was made as
early as the twelfth century by their
cousins the Celts of Ireland, and the presumption is that the art was known to their
common ancestors before the migration.
Distillation is mentioned by the Arab Geber,
who flourished about 800; but whether
Geber was known or not to the inhabitants
of mediæval Britain, it is unlikely that a
mere hint from him would, as some writers
have loosely and carelessly suggested, in-

spire the British Celts to the production of usquebagh. No doubt the art of distillation may have been discovered spontaneously by different nations, but it is entirely inconsistent with facts to theorise that the manufacture of whisky in Scotland originated in times comparatively modern through the introduction of the art of distillation from England or elsewhere. On the contrary, it is beyond question that usquebagh figured in the rude orgies of the Celtic clans long before modern influences had penetrated to their fastnesses. For centuries it may have remained wholly unknown to their Lowland neighbours: dammed up, as it were, by the barriers of alien custom and foreign speech. Hector Boece, who wrote about the beginning of the sixteenth century, says of the ancient customs of the Scots, that " at such times as they determined to be merry, they used a kind of *aqua vitæ* void of all spice, and only consisting of such herbs and roots as grew in their own gardens. Otherwise

their common drink was ale; but in time
of war, when they were enforced to lie in
camp, they contented themselves with
water, as readiest for their turns." Boece
is rather incorrect and credulous, and
many of his statements must be taken
cum grano salis; but his native district
bordered on the Highlands, and not im-
probably the Highland custom of drinking
usquebagh was occasionally indulged in
there, although himself appears to have
had a very indistinct and imperfect knowledge of the character of the liquor.

Possibly the first to introduce usquebagh
to the Lowlands were the monks; and, at
any rate, the earliest Lowlander associated
with its manufacture was a friar, John Cor
by name, who in 1495 obtained eight bolls
of malt from the exchequer for this purpose.
Its Latin name, *aqua vitæ,* also suggests
conventual associations. In 1505 the right
to sell it in Edinburgh was conferred on
the surgeons; and in 1557 Bessie Campbell
was summoned before the magistrates and

ordered to cease from vending it in the
burgh except on market days. The first
Scotsman handed down to posterity in
connection with a case of drunkenness from
whisky, was probably the ill-fated Darnley :
on one occasion he distinguished himself
by making one of his French friends drunk
on *aqua composita*, of the inebriating
qualities of which the Frenchman may
have been too sceptical. An enactment
that, by reason of the dearth of malt, no
whisky should be brewed or sold from the
1st of December, 1579, to the 1st of
December, 1580, except that nobles and
men of rank might distil it from their own
malt for use in their families, would seem
to prove that by that time the liquor was
advancing in popularity. It was much
earlier in general use in the west of Scotland than in other Lowland regions—a fact
which may be accounted for either by their
proximity to the Highlands or to the dis
tricts of the Strathclyde Welsh. Early
in the sixteenth century the inhabitants of

the western burghs—Ayr, Irvine, Glasgow,
Dumbarton—had liberty to furnish the
inhabitants of the isles with " baken bread,
brown ale, and *aqua vitæ*, in exchange for
other merchandise." In several towns and
burghs bordering on the Highland regions
whisky was distilled in considerable quantities early in the seventeenth century.
The principal indications of its Lowland
use at this time occur in the districts
fringing the Highlands, while the whole
weight of evidence leads to the conclusion
that its use in the latter region was universal. In 1616 the funeral expenses of
Sir Hugh Campbell of Calder amounted to
£1,647 16s. 4d., Scots, of which no less than
a fourth went in whisky ; while Taylor, the
Water Poet, refers to the " most potent
aqua vitæ " drunk at the great Highland
hunt meeting of 1618. In 1638 it was not
sold in the taverns of Aberdeen, " wine,
ale, or beer" being alone mentioned in a
regulation regarding their early closing ;
but along with ale or beer " strong waters

aqua vitæ" was in 1655 forbidden by the town council to be made or sold without a special license. By 1655 it was also sold in Glasgow taverns, and in 1657 a special day was appointed for fixing the excise on it.

In William Cleland's "Mock Poem upon the Highland Host who came to Destroy the Western Shires in Winter, 1678," the Gaelic love of whisky is specially satirised. "A tap horn filled with usquebay" is mentioned as one of the essential equipments of each; and, says Cleland, after cataloguing the "good things," which the Hielandman doth specially affect :—

> " There's something yet I have forgotten
> Which ye prefer to roast or sodden,
> Wine and wastles, I dare say,
> And that is routh * of usquebay."

In the Covenanting times usquebagh was contemned by the Presbyterians, both people and clergy ; but one of the accusa-

* Plenty.

tions brought in "Faithful Contendings" against three of the Covenanting preachers by the Covenanting General Hamilton was that "when at any time they came out to the country, whatever things they had, they were careful each of them to have a great flask of brandy with them, which was very heavy to some, particularly Mr. Cameron, Mr. Cargill, and Henry Hall."

By an Act of Parliament·of 1690, Duncan Forbes of Culloden, in recognition of his loyalty during the rebellion of Graham of Claverhouse, Viscount Dundee, and in consideration of the damage done to his lands and distillery of Ferintosh by the rebels, received a perpetual liberty to distil grain at his "brewery of *aqua vitæ* of Ferintosh" on payment of a small specific composition in lieu of excise. It is perhaps of importance to note that in this Act the brewery is styled "ancient," which would seem to indicate that whisky had been made at Ferintosh for at least a very considerable time, and probably long before

the property came into possession of the
Forbeses in 1670. The result of the grant
was to give Forbes almost a monopoly in the
manufacture of whisky, for which Ferintosh
continued to be a common synonym even
in the present century. In 1785 the
privilege was withdrawn, over £25,000
being paid in compensation. " Thee, Ferintosh! O sadly lost!" says Burns; and it
may well be believed that the moderate
price at which Ferintosh could be sold,
had greatly aided in popularising the liquor
in the Lowlands. Many a Lowlander had
doubtless learned to appreciate the merits
of usquebagh during the Highland cam-
paigns of Montrose and Dundee. Charles
Edward in his wanderings had frequently
to be content with it ; and on one occasion
he and two Highlanders finished a bottle
between them, the larger share falling to
the prince. At that period a " dram " was
the first article of hospitality presented to
a stranger on entering a Highland hut.
Not, however, till after the subjugation of

the Highlands and the amalgamation of
the two peoples, did whisky come to be
regarded as a Lowland Scottish drink. It
was not uncommon in the Lowlands, in the
time of the poet Fergusson, but he refers to
it as " Highland," and in " Leith Races "
associates whisky-drinking only with the
Highland guard of Edinburgh :—

> " To whisky pleuks * that burnt for 'oukst
> On Town-guard soldiers' faces,
> Their barber bauld his whittle ‡ crooks,
> An' scrapes them for the races."

For many years before whisky came into
general use brandy had been drunk by the
upper classes ; and among the Highland
gentry who affected the fashionable manners of the Lowlands brandy had almost
superseded their native liquor. In many
districts of the Lowlands the use of whisky
was also preceded by that of gin from
England or rum from Jamaica. In 1775
when Major Topham visited Edinburgh

* Pimples.   † Weeks.   ‡ Knife—Razor.

whisky was not a fashionable liquor. In the oyster cellars which he visited toddy appears to have been unknown. Punch was "quite the thing," but the choice was between brandy and rum punch. Rum was a specially favourite liquor in Glasgow (owing to its West Indian trade) at the close of the century : Strang, in his "Glasgow Clubs," states that "rum punch was the universal beverage of the members of the Pig Club at their dinners, as it was at those of all the jovial fraternities in the city ; and rum toddy was, as elsewhere, the accompaniment of every supper. Whisky in those days, being chiefly drawn from the large flat-bottomed stills of Kilbaggie Kennetpans, and Lochryan was only fitted for the most vulgar and fire-loving palates ; but when a little of the real stuff from Glenlivet or Arran could be got—and to get it was a matter of difficulty and danger—it was dispensed with as sparing a hand as curaçoa or benedictine."

The appearance of the modern public-

house on the scene of Scottish rural life
is chronicled by Hector MacNeill in his
" Will and Jean " (1795) :—

> " Brattling * down the brae, and near its
>   Bottom, Will first marv'lling sees
> ' Porter, Ale, and British Spirits,'
>   Painted bright between twa trees.
> ' Godsake, Tam, here's walth for drinking;
>   Wha can this new comer be ? '
> ' Hoot ! ' quo Tam, there's drouth in thinking—
>   Let's in, Will, and syne † we'el see.' "

Possibly Burns had considerable influence
in popularising whisky in Scotland.   He
mocked at those who wet " their weasan ‡
with liquors nice "; he railed at " brandy,
burning trash," and poured contempt on
" poor devils " who meddled " wi' bitter
dearthful wines "; and he patriotically ex-
tolled Scotia's native drink, the " barley
bree," whether in the form of ale, " the poor
man's wine," or in that of " whisky, soul
o' plays and pranks ! "   But ale is as
frequently the theme of his muse as the

---

* Hurrying.   † Then.   ‡ Windpipe, gullet.

stronger liquor. This was that "barley bree" that Willie, Rab, and Allan "preed the lee lang nicht"; and it was from "reaming swats that drank divinely" that Tam o' Shanter got courage to gaze unabashed on the "unco sight" in "Alloway's auld haunted kirk." Whether Burns's praise of liquor has had a prejudicial effect on Scottish life may be commended to the consideration of debating societies.

III.

THE population of Old-world Scotland being thin and sparse, the means of sustenance were on the whole plentiful. That was an exceptional household which, in the Middle Ages, and later, could not boast

"To haue guse, cok and hen,
  Bread, drink and bedding to treat horse and men."

Starvation, or even the mordant misery of hunger, was probably almost unknown, or the result of years unwontedly calamitous. Even when seasons were exceptionally unfavourable dearth was not so universal and all-pervading as to be intolerable; and though a course of Southron rapine might cause a vast amount of temporary suffering, it could hardly ruin the food resources of an entire district. A partial failure of the harvest might occasion some scarcity of bread, but probably what was affected was quality rather than quantity. In any case the staple vegetable, kale, retained its normal and luxurious greenness through all the atrocities of winter weather. Also when whole tracts were beggared of sheep and kine restitution was not impossible by means of a foray across the border; and in any case there were the moorlands and the woods, which abounded in game of many kinds, while the rivers and estuaries teemed unfailingly with fish. By the beginning of the sixteenth century the whole nation was not more than half a million strong; and although the science of agriculture was still in its infancy, it sufficed to meet such demands as were made on it. One dearth, serious in some parts of Scotland, did occur in the fifteenth century, but it was not till the closing half of the sixteenth century

that famine years recurred with any frequency. Even then much of the scarcity
was due to the luxurious living of the
nobles, or a result of the broils and civil
wars at the time of the Reformation or in
the reign of James VI. The farmer in early
times turned his attention chiefly to the
raising of oats, his sheep and cattle being
left almost wholly to their old ways and
their own devices; but dairy produce—
milk, butter, cheese—was in general use
from times the most remote. Barley and
wheaten bread were not uncommon at the
tables of the lords and barons, but from
time immemorial oats was the grain
affected by the multitude; and even yet
in Scotland a common synonym for it is
the generic term " corn."

At first, when the pinch of poverty was
not so sharp and flesh was cheaper and
more abundant, the grain was of less importance in itself, and the forms in which
it appeared were not so various; but oat-
cake was always the staple bread of Scot-

land, in the Lowlands and Highlands both.
"Of otes," according to Bishop Lesley's
"History of Scotland," "by the opinion of
many is made very gude bread, nocht taste-
less, but with great labour, quilke all the
north part of England, and the greater part
of Scotland use, and are sustained upon
commonly." In the north of England
the oaten cake was known as haver-bread,
and the same name was also current in
some parts of Scotland. "O whaur did ye
get that haver-meal bannock?" asked the
"silly auld body" of the ballad; and the
answer was, "Between St. Johnstone's"
(Perth) "and Bonnie Dundee." Writing
towards the close of the sixteenth century,
Fynes Moryson, as one illustration of the
rudeness of Scottish cookery, states that
the Scots "vulgarly" (commonly) "eat
hearth-cakes of oats." In Roman times
the same hearth-cakes of oats were the
bread of the savage natives, who baked
them on stones round the fire. These
stones the native Celts termed "greadeal."

They formed a ring round the fire, and
hence the peculiar significance of the word
" girdle " in the Scots vocabulary. Froissart has a curious reference to this ancient
and indispensable utensil of the Scottish
housewife, and gives a picturesque illustration of its use by the Scottish soldiers.
Amid all their wanderings and adventures
they remained ever faithful to their native
bread, and retained a tenderness almost
pathetic not for *aqua vitæ*, but for oatmeal.
It was the one indispensable article of
diet, and as they had no guarantee that
they would be able to beg, borrow, or steal
it, they had to carry with them a supply.
According to Froissart, a man's acoutre-
ments included a flat plate at his saddle
and a wallet of meal at his back, " the
purpose whereof is this: Whereas a Scottish
soldier hath eaten of flesh so long that he
begins to loathe the same, he casteth this
plate into the fire, he moisteneth a little
of his meal in water, and when the plate
is heated he layeth his paste thereon and

maketh a little cake the which he eateth
to comfort his stomach. Hence," our
author infers with a notion somewhat loose
and inexact of the principles of ethno-
logical or physiological science, "it is no
marvel that the Scots should be able to
make longer marches than other men."
All the same, if we are to believe the
anonymous author of "Andrew and his
Cutty Gun," oat-cakes might tend to bring
about a physical condition not altogether
conducive to the accomplishment of long
marches. Says he of his heroine, ale-wife,
or what-not :—

> "The carline * brought her kebbuck † ben
>   Wi' girdle-cakes well tosted broon.
> Weel does the canny kimmer ‡ ken, §
>   They gar‖ the scuds gae glither ¶ doon."

And annotating these stanzas—probably
for the information of benighted Southrons
—Burns remarks that "these oatmeal

| * Old woman. | † Cheese. | ‡ Gossip. |
| § Know. | ‖ Cause. | ¶ Easier. |

cakes are kneaded out with the knuckles and toasted over the red embers of wood on a gridiron. They are remarkably fine," he adds—presumably on the authority of frequent experience—"and a delicate relish when eaten warm with ale. On winter nights the landlady heats them and drops them into the quaigh to warm the ale." But if the muse of Allan Ramsay does not lie, the principle was absolute, for a pease scone might be substituted for the oaten cake :—

> " Sac brawly * did a pease-scon toast
> Biz i' the queff † and flie the frost,
> There we got fou wi' little cost
> And muckle speed."

It is possible that bannocks or scones— be they of wheat, or bere, or barley, or pease, or " mixed " meals—may point to the existence of a less primitive kitchen ; but they must nevertheless be reckoned as essentially Scottish. The differences in the

* Finely. † Drinking cup.

methods of baking and firing are mere adapta-
tions of old modes to the peculiarities of new
materials. Pease bread was very anciently
in use, but probably was only partaken of by
the poorest, or from dire necessity. Thus
in the "Lamentations of Lady Scotland,"
written in 1572 during the siege of the
Castle of Edinburgh, the extremity of
destitution is indicated in the line—

"And glaid to get Peis breid and watter caill."

Shortbread — "Scotch cake," as it is
called in South Britain—is probably the
triumph of Scottish baking on the old
national lines. It may have been the
invention of some professional Scotch cook
or baker, but he must at least have been
thoroughly imbued with the old Scots household notions in regard to the "staff of
life." It is probably entitled to the place
of honour among the breads of Britain, if
regard be had to the cheapness and simplicity of its materials, its pleasant sweet-

ness, and its wholesomeness and digestibility
in comparison to other sugared cates.

Among Scottish household breads neither
the wheaten loaf nor any form of wheaten
bread was ever included. These were (and
still are) known as "baker's bread," and
were only to be had in the principal towns.
It was enacted that sixteen ounces of fine
bread (doubtless the wheaten loaf) should
be supplied to Queen Mary's attendants for
four pennies Scots during her visit to Jedburgh in 1566; but even in cities, according to Fynes Moryson, wheaten bread was
bought, at the close of the sixteenth century, chiefly by "gentlemen, courtiers, and
the best kind of citizens." The records
of the burgh of Aberdeen contain a curious
enactment made on the 8th of October,
1656, forbidding, probably in the interests
of the professional baker, oat-cakes to be
baked or sold within the burgh, but
probably, in this instance at least, Aberdeen was in advance of other towns in
Scotland. As regards the country districts,

the wheaten loaf so late as 1750 was rarely seen on the tables even of the richer classes. " Though wheaten bread," says Dr. Somerville, " was partly used, yet cakes or bannocks of barley and peasemeal formed the principal household bread in gentlemen's families ; and in those of the middle class on ordinary occasions no other kind of bread was ever thought of." And thus, when railways were unknown and means of communication difficult in Scotland through, there prevailed a curious difference between town and country in respect of the bread in general use. Not more than fifty years back " loaf-bread " was still a luxury in certain districts, and the staple was as yet cakes or bannocks of oats or pease for the poorer classes, bannocks of barley-meal being used at the wealthier tables, and for special occasions at the tables of the poor. Thus a correspondent of Fergusson the poet promises to treat him, among other dainties " wi' bannocks o' gude barley-meal."

In the beginning the professional baker

in the towns may possibly have borrowed
his methods from the French. At any
rate, being patronised chiefly by the nobles
and the wealthier burghers, he was accustomed to use the very best materials,
and he rejoiced in every encouragement to
devote himself to the perfection of his
methods. Edinburgh was doubtless the
cradle of the craft ; and if you want
to beat the Edinburgh baker you must
go—not to London, but—to Paris or
Vienna. It is true that, with the accession of James VI. to the English throne,
London was invaded by a host of bakers,
among other tradesmen, from the north ;
but possibly the native shrewdness soon
perceived that to catch the obtuse, unedu-
cated English palate, it was as unneces-
sary to deal with the " finest of the
wheat " as to seek to excel in the art of
baking. At any rate their incursion has
failed to raise the average standard of
excellence of the London loaf, which is
probably the worst of any capital in Europe.

IV.

THE natural vegetable of Scotland was the green kale, of which nettles, leeks, onions, ranty-tanty (sorrel), carrots, and turnips were, most of them, probably late, and all of them certainly inadequate, and partial rivals. For unnumbered centuries the place of kale in Scottish domestic economy has been almost as unique as that of potatoes during the last two hundred years in the domestic economy of Ireland. A "gude kale-yaird" was as indispensable to the old Scottish cotter—and even his betters —as the potato-plot is to the Irish peasant.

> " Although my father was nae laird,
> 'Tis daffin * to be vaunty,†
> He keepit aye a gude kale-yaird,
> A ha' house and a pantry."

---

* Foolish.   † Boastful.

A recent writer on Ireland has bemoaned the adoption by the Irish of " Raleigh's fatal gift," which he describes as a " dangerous tuber " and a " demoralising esculent " ; but although the green kale has been in use in Scotland for unnumbered centuries, no suspicion of dangerous or demoralising tendencies have been mooted of it ; nor has it manifested any tendency unduly to " swell the population," except, perhaps, in a merely gastric sense. In ancient times every Scottish meal was flavoured with it in some form or other, great ingenuity being shown in varying the methods of its preparation. Both blades and stalks were utilised, nothing of the precious vegetable being discarded. A " Godly Song " has it that

" The monks of Melrose made good kaill
On Fridays when they fastit,"

which, being interpreted, means, that if they eschewed flesh, they at least did not scruple to make use of broth in which beef had been boiled. Even yet kale is the common name in Scotland for broth, and even a synonym for dinner.

Kale had thus in Scotland forestalled the potato, which in Ireland had become the chief and universal food of the masses before the end of the seventeenth century, but did not come into general use in "the land o' cakes" and kale till nearly a century later. For a long time the Scottish peasant's treatment of potatoes was curious and tentative. At first his view of them was probably identical with that of the housewife, who refused potatoes offered by a neighbour—they would "eat sae fine with the mutton," she said—on the ground that "we need nae provocatives in this house." He regarded them, that is, as less palatable than kale—or at least as a superfluity so long as kale was "to the fore"—and less nourishing than oatmeal; and when, towards the latter half of the eighteenth century, the farmer began planting them in the fields, there was a certain apprehension lest it should be attempted to substitute them, as in Ireland, for oatmeal, if not even for kale and beef. But, chiefly on account of its abundant yield, the potato was bound to win in the end, although the predilection of the Scot for it has never been so excessive as that of the Irishman. He has mastered it, indeed, as completely as the Irishman has been mastered by it; and he may now be said to have succeeded in making the most that can be made of it, whether as an article of diet or as a source of profit. Its fortune has somewhat modified the position of green kale, but the cotter's garden-plot is still the " kale-yaird," and the time-honoured vegetable has not been ousted from its place in the nation's esteem. It is needful, however, to explain that it was chiefly among the Lowlanders that kale attained its extraordinary vogue. It is a vegetable essentially Saxon and non-Celtic. The more unsophisticated Highlanders regarded its use as a symptom of effeminacy; the Grants

who, living near the Lowland line, had
grown fond of it were contemned as the
" soft kale-eating Grants," and a Gaelic
poem on the battle of Killiecrankie mocks
at Mackay's defeated soldiers as " men of
kale and brose." When the Highlander
indulged in such a luxury as broth he
preferred the common nettle; and, indeed,
it was somewhat appropriate to the cateran. As for the aboriginal mountaineer,
his appetite for vegetables was fed chiefly
on wild fruits and nuts, the roots of wild
herbs, and the leaves of certain trees.

In the very early centuries oats and kale
were probably far less important staples of
diet among the poorer classes than they
subsequently became. In the case of
Europeans vegetarianism, like teetotalism,
is essentially a modern fad, chiefly affected
by persons more or less languid and un-
healthy morally or physically. A vigorous
and energetic race is always carnivorous,
and in later times it was simply the
scarcity of flesh that compelled the Scottish

peasant to feed on it so sparingly. The aboriginal cave-dwellers were beyond doubt great eaters of flesh, and as long as it abounded it must have formed the chief food of the whole community. Abundant it seems to have been till at least the sixteenth century. Bishop Lesley records of the Bordermen of his time that they made very little use of bread, living chiefly upon flesh, milk, and cheese, and sodden barley. The northern Highlanders, who also were marauders, ate flesh largely, and often ate it raw. Lesley, indeed, affirms that they preferred it dripping with blood, because it was then "mair sappie and nourishing"; but his information on the point appears to have been defective, for though they did frequently eat beef and venison raw, their custom was to prepare it by squeezing the slices dry between wooden battens. One reason for this ultra-savage style of feeding was probably the original scarcity of cooking utensils, for the Highlander's antipathy to the arts of the craftsman was inveterate. When the aboriginal Highlander or Borderer did condescend to cook his dinner, his appliances were of the simplest: he contented himself with seething the flesh of the animal in its own paunch, or in its skin. The brue, or broth, obtained in this way was the common drink of the Highlander; and Lesley affirmed it to have been so excellent that not the best wine, nor any other kind of drink, might be compared to it. Probably its quality was very similar to that of the strong Lowland soup called skink.

To the Highlander's habit of battening himself on raw flesh may probably be traced the tradition that now and then he was addicted to cannibalism. (The men of Annandale were also famed for similar dietetic eccentricities.) No doubt the calumny—if calumny it were—obtained a wider and more permanent acceptance by reason of the fact that the authority of St. Jerome could be quoted in support of it. But, calumny or not, it had gained

such credence, even in Jacobite times, in
England that when the outlandish host
appeared across the border some nervous
folk were seriously concerned lest they or
any of theirs should be ravished away to
grace some conqueror's board.

As a matter of fact, the ancient Highlander, or at least the Highlander of the
later Middle Ages, was very temperate in
food and drink. No doubt he now and
then indulged in frantic "spreeing," especially after a more than commonly successful
foray; but as a rule he despised luxury
and eschewed both gluttony and drunkenness. He broke his fast with a light meal,
and took nothing more till in the evening
he dined in the great hall of his chief.
Here the character and quality of the food
provided were regulated to some extent by
the rank of the guest. But all ate sparingly; corpulence—*pace* Sir John Falstaff
an inconvenient endowment for the professional thief—being held in high abhor-
rence.

V.

In the Lowlands it was, in early times, the custom of the nobles to entertain the bulk of their dependants at a common table. "Great families," says Lesley, " they feed, and that perpetually, partly to defend themselves from their neighbours, with whom they have daily feud, partly to defend the realm"; for the power and influence of the noble depended largely on the number and lustihood of his followers. Hospitality to strangers, too, was regarded as a sacred duty; so much so that when taverns began to be substituted, special enactments were passed compelling travellers to lodge at least their servants in them. Hunting

being a chief pastime in years of peace,
there was never a lack of venison and wild
game. Herds of wild cattle ranged the
Caledonian forest, but such was "the
gluttony of man" (the flesh of the animal,
though "all grissillie," being of "a trim
taste") that by the sixteenth century
their numbers had been greatly diminished.
Another kind of "ky nocht tame," with
flesh of a "marvellous sweetness, of a
wonderful tenderness, and excellent deli-
cateness of taste" (the breed was doubtless
the long-horned Highland) ranged the
hill-country of Argyll and Ross almost at
will. Besides other winged game, laver-
ocks were a common article of diet, being
in some districts so plentiful that in the
sixteenth century twelve were sold for a
French sou. Rabbits, or "cunyies," were
such a favourite dish that in the thirteenth
century a warren and its warrener were
attached to every burgh. Mutton was in
more common use than beef, but cows were
kept in great numbers for dairy purposes,

and the monks were great poultry masters
and encouragers of husbandry. In some
parts there were swine that the forests
glutted with mast and acorns, but otherwise they seem to have led a somewhat
unhappy and persecuted life. Sir Walter
states that "pork or swine flesh in any
shape was till of late years much abomi-
nated by the Scots, nor is it yet a favourite
dish amongst them." No doubt the latter
clause of this pronouncement was true
when Sir Walter wrote, but the former
requires modification. The antipathy of
the ancient Highland Scot to pork was as
marked as the Jews, but among Lowlanders
the distaste was neither so general nor so
decided. From time immemorial pigs have
been kept in the Lowlands. They seem to
have been at least occasionally kept by the
monks; a charter of David I. to the Abbey
of Holyrood contains the following provision : "And the swine, the property of
the aforesaid church, I grant in all my
woods to be quit of pannage." This was,

however, before luxury had affected the
ancient monastic habit. For many generations pork was in all probability the food
chiefly of the serfs and the poorer classes
generally. This may even be inferred from
the severity of the enactments against their
depredations. Thus, while other animals
might only be impounded in such cases,
swine found eating the corn or rooting in
the tilth might be slain out of hand. But
although at intervals from 1450 the town
council of Edinburgh continued to order
all swine found in the open streets, closes,
or vennels of the city to be slaughtered or
escheated, these industrious wayfarers went
on contributing their quota to the picturesqueness and vivacity of street life in the
capital till as late as the close of the
eighteenth century. The swine—magiste-
rially described as "ane unseemlie kind of
beast"—does not seem to have invaded
the city of Aberdeen until the middle of
the seventeenth century. But it also ex-
hibited there the same inveterate love of

city life. Dr. Somerville states that in his
time, "though pork was sometimes presented at table, few ate of it when fresh,
and even when cured it was not generally
acceptable." Nevertheless it had begun to
be exported in 1703, and an Act of 1705
for encouraging exportation contains direc-
tions for curing and packing. No doubt
the introduction of the potato has greatly
aided the extension of pig-keeping; and
the change in the fashion of breakfasting
introduced by the use of tea and coffee has
given pork a permanent and prominent
place at Scots as well as English tables.

Fish, both freshwater and salt, were
largely used as food in Scotland from the
thirteenth century onwards. The monks
especially were devoted to the fostering
and development of fisheries; and it was
chiefly owing to their guidance and encouragement that the industry was soon a
source of national wealth. By the thirteenth century Aberdeen was famous for
her speldrins and other dried fish. As for

Loch Fyne herrings, "In no place," says
Lesley, "were herrings so fat and of so
pleasant a taste as in that loch"; and long
before the bishop's time their peculiar
excellence had secured them a ready sale
in foreign parts. The salmon fishery, however, was probably the most important of
all. The abundance of salmon in Scottish
rivers is proverbial, the reason being no
doubt that clearness of the water which
comes of sandy or stony courses. This
abundance caused salmon to be at one
time despised by the wealthier classes in
Scotland; and even in the eighteenth
century so plentiful was the fish in some
districts of Perthshire that the hinds made
stipulations reducing the frequency of its
appearance on the bill of fare.

The virtues of the oyster were early
recognised. He figured along with buckies,
limpets, partans, crabs, and other shell-fish
at the royal banquet at Stirling in 1594,
on the occasion of the baptism of Prince
Henry; but not till long afterwards did

he become a fashionable luxury. Thus
" glaikit * fools ower rife o' cash " were
" pampering their wames † wi' fulsome
trash," while Fergusson, with the poet's
discernment, was inditing odes to him—

> " The halesomest and nicest gear
> O' fish or flesh,"

and was prescribing him as one of the chief
of medicines for mind or body—

> " Come prie,‡ frail man, for gin thou'rt sick,
>   The oyster is a rare cathartic
> As ever doctor patient gart § lick
>   To cure his ails ;
>   Whether you hae the head or heart ache
>   It aye prevails."

It were hard to tell for how many ages
the cry of " Caller oo "ᵢ‖ has been skirled
through Edinburgh, but it is safe to say
that the most ancient houses in High
Street are younger than those which echoed
back the first " agreeable wild notes " of
the " great mother" of the noble Newhaven

---

* Careless. † Bellies. ‡ Taste.
§ Caused. ‖ Fresh oysters.

succession. In the eighteenth century
supping in oyster cellars was a fashionable
diversion of Edinburgh ; and Major Topham, in his "Letters from Edinburgh"
(1776), remarks that the oyster cellar,
named by its votaries the "Temple,"
seemed "to give more real pleasure to
the company who visit it than either
Ranelagh or the Pantheon." At such
entertainments the presence of ladies was
not merely allowable, but almost essential.
Oyster suppers would not appear to have
yet become an institution in English towns,
and the Major naïvely confesses that after
partaking of the fare he sat "waiting in
expectation of a repast that was never to
make its appearance" till all else was forgotten in the excellence of the brandy
punch and the charming conversation of
the ladies, "who," he remarks, "to do
them justice, are much more entertaining
than their neighbours in England," and
"discovered a great deal of vivacity and
fondness of repartee."

Mussels, the oyster's poor relation, were probably consumed as early as the Roman period in the form of mussel-brose. At any rate the burgh of that name is supposed to have been a Roman station; nor is there any doubt that its fame and fortune, like those of Newhaven, are based upon shell-fish.

> "At Musselbrough, an' eke* Newhaven
> The fisher-wives will get top livin'
> When lads gang out on Sunday's even
> To treat their joes, †
> An' tak' o' fat pandores a prieven ‡
> Or mussel-brose."

Thus the veracious Fergusson; and how long the custom he describes existed before it found its appropriate muse eludes research.

* Likewise.   † Sweethearts.   ‡ Tasting.

VI.

THERE can be no doubt that in their fashions
of living the Scots nobility were largely
biassed by the influence of France. According to George Buchanan, luxury had
begun to affect the national habit as early
as the reign of David I., though that king,
he states, was moved to banish his kingdom
all epicures and such as studied to titilate
and provoke the appetite. There is abundant evidence that the magnificent feasts
and banquetings which were characteristic
of the Middle Ages were not neglected by
the Scottish monarchs, and it would moreover appear that gradually a very special
attention was devoted in Scotland to

cookery. Hector Boece laments that where previously there was "plenty with sufficiency, we have immoderate courses with superfluity, as he war maist noble and honest that could devore and swell maist, and be extreme diligence serchis so mony deligat courses that they provoke the stomach to ressave more than it may sufficiently digest." These and other "new ingynis and devysis," he further states, were introduced by the nobility, " efter the fassione quhilke they have seen in France." That the modes of cookery were considerably modified by the French alliance may also be inferred from the names for some principal dishes, though these, whatever their style and title, may of course be of purely native origin. We learn from the Exchequer Rolls that James I. kept a French cook, and the probability is that his successors did likewise. That James IV. was as addicted to the pleasures of the table as to the splendour and magnificence of the

tournament may be inferred from Dunbar's
"Dirge to the King bydand [abiding] to
lang in Stirling." Parodying the ritual of
the Church, the poet invokes the aid of
patriarchs, prophets, apostles, saints, and
martyrs for the deliverance of his master
from the purgatorial "distress of Stirling
town," and his restoration to the heavenly
"merriness" of Edinburgh.

> " Ye may in hevin heir with us dwell
> To eit swan, cran, pertik, and plever,
> And every fische that swims in rever ;
> To drynk with us the new fresche wyne
> That grew upon the rever of Ryne ;
> Ffresche fragrant clairettis out of France
> Of Angerss and Orléance
> With mony ane course of gryt dyntie.
> Say ye amen for cheritie."

According to Buchanan, his successor
James V. was temperate in his diet and
seldom drank wine, but his personal habits
in this respect had little effect on the customs of the time. During a great hunt in
the Highlands he was himself entertained
by the Earl of Atholl with (according to

Lindsay of Pitscottie) "all sich delicious
and sumptuous meattis as was to be hade
in Scotland, for fleschis, fischis, and all
kindis of fyne wyne, and spyces, requisit for
ane prince." An interpolated passage in a
later manuscript than that mainly followed in
the printed edition of Lindsay's "Chronicle"
is touched with more particularity, and
notes that " Syne were ther proper stuards,
cunning baxters, excellent cooks and potin-
garis, with confections and drugs for their
disserts." Under James's widow, Mary of
Guise, French fashions continued to pre-
vail at table as elsewhere, and under her
daughter, Mary Stuart, the French tradition
was unimpaired. Knox makes special reference to the extravagant banqueting of
both the queen and her nobles. " The
effairis of the kytcheing," he sardonically
explains, "were so gryping that the mynes-
teris stipendis could nocht be payit." When
Mary visited Jedburgh in 1566 the Privy
Council passed a regulation that " ane
manns ordinar at the melteth, being servit

with bruise, beef, mutton, and rost at the
least, should be sixteen pennies Scotch";
and this was no doubt the servants' ordinary. The "rost"—the French *rôti*—
probably consisted of some kind of game,
but the brose no doubt was kale-brose, and
the sodden beef and mutton are distinctly
Scots. Presumably the viands served to
the nobles and courtiers were much more
sumptuous in quality.

That the French system of courses had
come into general use is evident from a law
of 1581 against "superfluous banqueting,"
which provided under certain prescribed
penalties that no archbishop, bishop, nor
earl should have more than eight dishes of
meat at a meal; no abbot, lord, prior, nor
dean more than six; no baron nor free-
holder more than four; and no burgher
nor other substantious spiritual or temporal
more than three. The Act was not to apply
to certain festival days nor to banquets to
foreigners, which latter, however, were only
to be given by archbishops, lords, abbots,

deans, barons, and provosts. Another Act
was passed against the use of "foreign
drugs or confections"; and the reason of
the enactments against luxury was that
food supplies were actually beginning to
run short. More than half a century before
Dunbar had lamented that

> "In burghis to landward and to sie
> Quhair was pleasure and grit plentie,
> Vennysann, wyld-fowll, wynne, and spice
> Ar now decayed through covetyce."

The treatment of waste and luxury was
no doubt a first symptom of the disease,
but the increase of population and the
backwardness of agriculture and cattle-
rearing made that disease worse felt as
years went on. The Acts (passed in different years) prohibiting meat during Lent,
and latterly also on Wednesdays, Fridays,
and Saturdays, were professedly occasioned
by the prevailing dearth; and to some extent their influence continued down to the
eighteenth century. Thus the bursars of

St. Andrew's University, so long as they continued to dine in the Common Hall, were restricted three days of the week to fish and eggs, and to broth and beef on the other four. In Aberdeen the sin or crime of "superfluous banquetting" seems to have been besetting at baptisms. In 1626 the Town Council of the granite city deemed it expedient to enact "that thair shall be bot sex women at the most invited or employed to convey the child to and fra the kirk, nather yet shall thair be any man persons invited to any denner supper or afternoones drink at a baptisme, or yit any other tyme during the haill space of the womanes chyldbed, or at the upseat bot sex men and sex women at the most: And withal ordaines that naine presume to have at any such tyme any kynd of suggars droiges or confectionns brocht from foraine countreis, nather yit any kynd, of vennesone wyld meat or baikin meat under the pain of fourtie poundes money." The Reformers inculcated austerity in diet

persistently ; and erroneous and even
baneful as were their notions in regard
to the sinfulness attaching to most forms
of enjoyment, some of the restrictions
imposed by them may have been salutary
for the nonce. By especially discountenan-
cing extravagance and wastefulness among
the wealthy they possibly to some extent
succeeded in preventing the want of food
from pressing too severely on the poorer
classes. Moreover to those whose means
of procuring food were limited it was doubtless a certain comfort to reflect that there
was virtue in abstinence. One peculiar
innovation of Protestantism was the introduction of an uncommon form of fasting.
The general practice of that form "of
private fasting which standeth chiefly in a
temperate diet" was recommended as of
special religious efficacy; and in the "Order
of the General Fast" appointed by the
General Assembly of the Kirk in 1565
there was ordained a week's "perishing,"
during the whole of which only the most

meagre diet was permissible, while entire
abstinence was "commanded to be from Setterday at eight houres at night till Sunday
after the exercise at afternoone, that is after
five houres ; and then only bread and drink "
[water, no doubt] "and that with great
sobriety." As a protest or reaction against
current excesses such a form of discipline
may not have been altogether ineffectual
for good, though human nature—even that
variety bred in Caledonia "stern and wild "
—was bound in the long run to find it " too
grievous to be borne."

VII.

THE great change in the Scots kitchen dates from the beginning of the seventeenth century. It was a consequence partly of the severance of intercourse with France, partly of the Puritanism of the Reformers, and partly of the increasing insufficiency of the supplies of meat. In all probability it was during the next hundred and fifty years that oaten meal, always an important article of diet, became almost exclusively the food of many districts. When Fynes Moryson visited Scotland in 1598 the servants at the knight's table dined on porridge, but each plate had in it a piece of sodden meat. As

times grew harder porridge was still the
staple, but (here the italics are absolute)
the piece of sodden meat had vanished.
Thus, too, the important ingredient in the
ancient kale soup was less the kale "broo"
than the beef-juice; but in later and harder
years there was but kale and *water*. Frequently the make-believe of water-kale, or
" muslin-kale," as Burns has it, was supped
instead of the original broth even in Henry-
son's time, the latter half of the fifteenth
century—

> " Thus how he stands in labour and bondage,
>   That scantlie may he purchcs by his maill
>   To leve upon dry-breid and water-caill."

In the austerer years of the seventeenth
and eighteenth centuries the French influence was discernible chiefly in the ingenuity displayed by the housewife in
making the most of nothing. The " Blythe-
some Bridal " is comparatively well-known,
but some lines of it may here be quoted as
a complete exposition of the kitchen of

lower-class Scotland in the seventeenth century :—

> " And there'll be lang kale and pottage,
> And bannocks o' barley meal,
> And there'll be guid saut herrin'
> To relish a cogue * o' guid yill.
>
> *   *   *   *   *
>
> Wi' siybows and rifarts and carline
> That are baith sodden and raw.
>
> *   *   *   *   *
>
> There'll be tartan, dragen and brochan,
> And fouth o' guid gabbocks o' skate,
> Powsoudie, and drammock, and crowdie,
> And caller nowt-feet on a plate.
> And there'll be partans and buckies,
> And speldins and haddocks enew,
> And singit sheep-heads and a haggis,
> And scadlips to sup tell ye're fou.
>
> There'll be lapper-milk keppocks,
> And sowens, and farles and baps,
> Wi' swats and weel-scraped paunches,
> And brandy in stoups and in caups ;
> And there'll be meal-kail and custocks
> Wi' skink to sup till ye rive,
> And roasts to roast on a brander
> Of flouks that were taken alive.

               * Wooden jug.

Scrapt haddocks, wilks, dulse and tangle,
And a mill o' guid sneeshin to prie;
When weary wi' eatin' and drinkin'
We'll rise up and dance till we dee."

Apart from the abundance of fish, the special feature of the " Brydal " banquet is the metamorphoses of meal. " Bannocks o' barley meal " (the finest bread of the lower classes) figure prominently enough. But of oatmeal we have tartan—tartan purry it was sometimes called, and probably therefore was a partially French invention—a pudding made chiefly of chopped kale and oatmeal ; brochan—oatmeal mixed with boiled water, flavoured with onions or pounded cheese ; drammock—raw meal and water ; crowdie—a thicker variety of the same with the addition of butter, or possibly milk porridge, sometimes called crowdie-mowdy ; meal-kail—the " Kail-brose o' auld Scotland " ; with " sowens," " farles," " baps," and, to crown all, the haggis. The white and red puddings are absent, " weel-scraped paunches " (or tripe) being favoured

in their stead; and wisely, for they could
but have been at a discount in the radiant
presence of the "great chieftain o' the
Puddin-race." Certain benighted and God-
forsaken theorists have ventured to surmise
(from the similarity of the name to the
French "hachis") that the haggis is one
of the nobler legacies of France to Scotland; and of course it is possible that
some earlier Vatel, some prehistoric Soyer,
crowned the preparation with its un-Scot-
tish name. But the oatmeal is peculiarly
Scottish; and the method of cooking is not
very far removed from the early barbarism
of using the paunch of the animal as its
own seething pot. Moreover, to the French
themselves the haggis is *le pain bénit
d'Écosse.* (It was frequently eaten cold;
and doubtless owed its designation, "*le pain
bénit,*" to the fact that it was customary to
send it from the old country to the "Scot
abroad.") That the haggis was suggested
rather by thrifty poverty than by epicurean
daintiness seems also antecedently prob-

6

able. Even in Dunbar's day its satisfying
bounteousness had become proverbial—

> "The gallowes gapes efter thy graceless gruntle,*
> As thou would for a haggeis, hungry gled."

In the peasant's home it was set in the
centre of the table, all gathering round it
with their horn spoons; and it was "deil
tak' the hindmost," or (as the proverb has
it) the haggis was "gaen gear."

Other specially Scots dishes mentioned
in the "Brydal" *menu* are caller nowt-feet,
or ox's feet; powsowdie (sheep's-head
broth), singed sheep's-heads—all no doubt
formerly despised by the rich noble, and
therefore regarded as very much the perquisite of the poor. Thus—

> "A haggis fat,
> Weel tottled in a seething pat,"

a sheep's-head with four black trotters,
"guid fat brose," and—

* Snout.

" White and bloody puddins routh
To gar the doctor skirl o' drouth,"

constitute the bill of fare which Fergusson
(who did not love the scorner of Scotland)
would have provided for the banquet to Dr.
Johnson given in the University of St.
Andrew's in 1773. The soups at the
" Brydal " feast were powsowdie, already
mentioned, scadlips—hot water judiciously
tempered with barley—and skink (no doubt
made from the before-mentioned " caller
nowt-feet "). Scotch broth, or kale (of
which originally the principal ingredients
were " knockit," or broken barley and kale :
peas, onions, &c., being later additions and
debasements "), is absent, only meal-kail
being mentioned. Beef has no place at
the banquet, and mutton appears only in
the form of the " singit sheep's-heads "
afore alluded to. In some counties—Fife,
for instance—preparations of oatmeal and of
kale—without beef—were for many years
the main diet of the peasantry—

" When cog o' brose an' cutty * spoon
Is a' our cottar childis boou,
Wha thro' the week till Sunday's speal †
Toil for pease cods and gude lang kail."

But in more inland counties, such as Perth
and Stirling, meat continued in more or less
general use up to the present time, broth
and beef being the ordinary dinner even of
the farm servants.

Ancient Scottish cookery was specially
distinguished by the excellence and variety
of its soups. Of these it may suffice to
mention three : to wit, hotch-potch, cockie-
leekie, and specially fish-soup, compared to
which last the greasy turtle-broth of London
City is a gross and barbarous abomination.
The roasting of beef or mutton was not
common till times comparatively recent,
boiling and stewing being the favourite
methods, except (as France had dictated) in
the case of fowls. Dr. Somerville states
that in his early days there was no roasting-
jack, but the spit was turned by one of the

* Short   † Rest.

servants or by a dog that had been trained
to manage a big wooden wheel. The essential difference between Scottish and English
modes of dining is well exemplified in the
story of an Aberdeen "baillie." This
worthy, returning from a brief sojourn in
London, was congratulated on his appearance. Resenting the impeachment with a
certain bitterness he expressed surprise that
it should be so, " for," quoth he, "deil a
speen was i' ma mou a' the time I was
awa'." Even in Fergusson's day, however,
Scottish modes of dining had begun to be
affected by English influences, and roast beef
was fast winning to its present pride of place.
With rather unpatriotic forgetfulness of the
" warm-reckin' " richness of the "haggis
fat, weel tottled in a seething pat," this
poet, forsaking his native Doric, salutes the
conqueror in the following mock-heroic
strains :—

> " Hail, Roast Beef ! monarch of the festive throng,
> To hunger's bane the strongest antidote ;
> Come, and with all thy rage-appeasing sweets

Our appetite allay ; for, or attended
By root Hibernian or plum-pudding rare,
Still thou art welcome to the social board."

Burns, on the other hand, would

"Gie dreeping roasts to countra lairds
Till icicles hang frae their beards " ;

but as he adds in the same breath—

" An' yill an' whisky gie to cairds *
Until they scunner † "

the seriousness of his scorn is open to
question.

* Tinkers.   † Loathe.

VIII.

In Scotland the free and open hospitality which bespeaks a primitive condition of society survived much later than in the better civilised parts of Europe. With a hostile England on her southern marches, she occupied a situation peculiarly isolated from foreign influences. The establishment of trading communities was also sadly discouraged by repeated invasions from England, which confined commercial intercourse almost entirely to certain of her sea-coast towns. Even when no active hostilities were afoot her trade with England was extremely limited during the whole period anterior to the union. Thus, although the

Scot himself was known as scholar or soldier
in many lands, it was but rarely that Scottish ground, except in the case of an English
raid, was trodden of foreign foot.   In Edinburgh and other cities frequented by the
Court, a tincture of French elegance and
refinement imparted a certain bizarre effect
to the essential rudeness of the national
habit ; but even here the alien influence did
not penetrate beyond a very narrow circle.
The inland regions, sparse in population and
devoid of trade, had scarce any intercourse
with the towns—they. were self-supporting
and self-dependent.   Travellers were mostly
one or other species of beggar—pilgrims,
poor scholars, friars, bards, minstrels, mounte-.
banks, sorners ; for, as the industrial part
of the rural community enjoyed an absolute fixity of tenure, few of its members
had friends or relatives at any distance from
their own homes, while such wayfarers as
were not beggars were chiefly nobles bound
for the castles of their brethren, or for the
great hunting gatherings which formed in

times of peace their chief occupation and
amusement. The commonest resort for
lodgings was either the guest-house of the
monastery or the noble's mansion; accommodation and cheer being regulated by
the qualities and conditions of the guests.
Except in famine years, a rude abundance
prevailed throughout the land until at least
the fifteenth century; and as rushes, straw,
fern, or heather were deemed sufficient and
even luxurious bedding by the majority, the
housing of strangers was attended with small
inconvenience.

The earliest recorded instance of legislative interference on behalf of travellers is
an Act of David II., in 1357. The accommodation to be secured by it must have
been extremely rude and humble. It provided that in every burgh the sellers of
bread and ale should " receive passengers in
herbery within their houses," and sell them
provisions at the prices enacted from neigh
bours. All such as refused full payment
might be apprehended in the king's name

by "the community of the burgh," which
was not to be held responsible for any injury
inflicted on the defaulter during his arrest-
ment (a very complete bill of immunity).
The Act of James I. (1424) was more comprehensive in scope. It decreed that in
burghs and thoroughfares hostelries should
be provided with accommodation and food
for man and beast; the intention clearly
being the provision of better lodging and
entertainment than could be had at the
alehouses. As regards the opening of
hostelries, the Act appears to have been
effectual; the difficulty consisting in making
them popular. In the following year the
new-made hosts, having waited in vain for
custom, presented a grievous complaint to
the king against the "villanous" practice of
travellers in putting up at the houses of
their friends. All travellers on foot or
a-horseback were thereupon prohibited from
lodging elsewhere than at the inn, special
exception being made in the case of those
with large retinues, who, however, were

bound to send their followers and servants
to the inn. But the ancient custom of free
hospitality survived many such enactments,
and, passing through long and gradual stages
of extinction, died very hard. In the sixteenth century the " hosteller without the
town " of Berwick-on-Tweed, in the eyes of
the Scots author of " The Friars of Berwick," was " wonder good " (by contrast, no
doubt, with those in Scotland proper); but
it seems to have been seldom frequented for
lodging, and the bed for the wearied friars
was " intill one loft was made for corn
and hay." There was an attempt to re-
vive the old Acts regarding inns in 1567;
but, so far as the general establishment of
suitable hostelries was concerned, they continued to remain a dead letter for two
centuries more. Fynes Moryson, in 1589,
" did never see nor hear that they have any
public inns with signs hanging out " (a picturesque feature of the English villages),
" but the better sort of citizens brew ale,
the usual drinke (which will distemper a

stranger's body), and the same citizens
entertain passengers on acquaintance or
entreaty." Plainly the attitude of the
taverners towards strangers savoured somewhat of a supercilious independence. Eighty
years after Moryson, Thomas Kirke testifies
to an exactly similar state of matters.
"The Scots," he says, "had not inns but
change-houses (as they call them), poor,
small cottages, where you must be content
to take what you find." By this he meant
that there was absolutely no choice of
dishes in the *menu*. What he did find was
"perhaps eggs with chicks in them and
some lang kale; at the better sort of them
a dish of chapped chickens" (probably
cocky-leeky). As to the enticements of the
latter delicacy, we may turn to Burt, who
crossed the border in the year of grace
1725; only we must substitute pigeons—
no doubt esteemed a special luxury—for
chickens. "The cloth," says Burt, "was
laid, but I was too unwilling to grease my
fingers to touch it, and presently after the

pot of pigeons on the table. When I came
to examine my cates, there were two or
three of the pigeons lay mangled in the
pot." In objecting to the " mangling " Burt
does but betray the Southron benighted-
ness ; but the mark of " dirty fingers in the
butter" was a touch he may be pardoned
for failing to appreciate. It is but fair to
add that, while the ineffable filthiness of
the bed-curtains almost debarred him from
making trial of his bed, he was agreeably
disappointed to find—as he did throughout
Scotland—that the linen was " white, well
aired, and hardened." Dr. Somerville, a
native Scot, testifies, some time after the
experiences of Burt, that there was little
improvement. In his youthful days " few
inns were to be met with in which the
traveller could either eat or sleep with
comfort ; and so ill-provided were they
with the most necessary articles, that on a
journey people used to carry a knife and
fork in a case deposited in the side-pocket
of their small-clothes." Glasses were so

scarce that a single one usually went round the whole company; and, as the said company was frequently very heterogeneous, it is plain that to fastidious persons, if any such there were, the act of drinking would not be one of unalloyed delight. The presiding genius of the change-house, or inn, was the ale-wife, or " brewster-wife," as she was called, who assumed a position of entire equality with her guests, and in taverns of the better class expected to be asked to take a glass of wine with them when that liquor was dispensed.

A century ago Edinburgh herself was no better off than the country districts in the matter of inns. In 1776, according to Major Topham, she had "no inn that is better than an alehouse, nor any accommodation that is decent, cleanly, or fit to receive a gentleman." In the "best inn in the metropolis" (situate in the Pleasance), the bare-legged waitress, in short gown and petticoat, informed him and his companion that "we could have no beds,

unless we had an inclination to sleep together and in the same room with the
company which a stage-coach had that
moment discharged." Information of a
like kind is still sometimes given in the
height of the tourist season to travellers in
Scotland; but the arrangements at which
the Major stood aghast were chronic and
perpetual in the hostelry of the Pleasance :
the old common guest-chamber of ancient
times was still a fact. A glimpse of the
Highland hotel of the period is afforded in
Ramsay's " Scotland and Scotsmen of the
Eighteenth Century." The original Highland innkeeper would appear to have more
than vied with his Lowland brother in
" pride, sloth, and dirtiness." Communica-
tions couched in terms with any semblance
to command were resented as a serious
breach of manners on the part of the visitor,
the inn being regarded as the host's " own
house." Thus a Southron lady, who had
been too inconsiderate of the feelings of
a sometime duniwassel, discovered, to her

dismay, that "both inkeeper and servants had disappeared on the eve of dinner." Possibly the traditional "Highland pride" still lingers within the precincts of a few Highland hostelries ; and occasionally, at least, the "Highland hunger" is manifested in the bill.

IX.

The "sorners and masterful beggars" against whom special proceedings were instituted by King James I. of Scotland in the first half of the fifteenth century, have their analogues to-day in the colonial settlements of Australia and New Zealand; and the presumption is that they were the product of similar social and economic conditions. Like the most of their modern cousins, the Scots "sorners" were ostensibly sportsmen; and, according to the Acts for their suppression, they were lords of "horses and hounds." The chances are they most abounded in districts where game abounded also; but it is not unlikely that a favourite diversion was a border foray, and that, having thus acquired a distaste for the monotonies of husbandry, they had little other means of support, when forays failed them and the pungent delights of cattle-lifting were impossible, than that of "sorning" on the less romantic but more exemplary section of the community. Their practice was simply a prostitution of the traveller's privilege according to the immemorial rites of hospitality. It may have been coeval in origin with those rites, for abuse is nearly always coincident with use; but the growing scarcity of the necessities of life, while it made the visits of these ambiguous guests more and more unwelcome, tended also in a nearly equal ratio to multiply them. The Acts for the suppression of vagabonds and sorners must therefore be taken as indicating that by the middle of the fifteenth century increase of population had effected such a change in economic conditions that the ancient custom of free hospitality was beginning to be a serious burden. By the Act of 1449 the horses, hounds, and other chattels of such as were convicted of being "sorners and masterful beggars" were escheated to the king, and the masterful ones themselves were to be held in ward until the king declared his will. In the same Act mention is made of persons "who made themselves fooles, who were not bards, or such-like runners about"; which feigned fools were evidently an inferior order to the "sorners," for they were dealt with much more summarily. If "any were found" they were to be "imprisoned or put in irons and detained as long as they had anything of their own to live upon, and after this was consumed," pursues the Act (with more of cruelty than grammar), "then their ears were to be nailed to the trone and cut off, and banished out of the country," and "afterwards if they be found in the kingdom they shall be hanged." In an Act of 1457, however, all "sorners, bards, masterful beggars, and feigned fools" are lumped

together as alike noxious and equally merit-
ing the common meed of punishment.

These references to a class of mendicant
bards are worth considering. The bard's
position in the household of the Highland
chieftain was recognised and honourable.
Buchanan mentions that even in his day
they were held in so great honour that in
some districts their persons were accounted
sacred and their houses sanctuaries; and
that even when clans were at open war
with each other the bards and their retinue
were allowed to pass and repass at their
pleasure. In Lowland Scotland the place
and prerogative of the bard's vocation are
more obscure. George Martine in his
" Reliquiæ Divi Andreæ " (1683) makes
mention of a class of beggar-bards called
" Jockies," who in his time wandered the
country through reciting " sloggorne or
war cries." When he wrote there were
said to be not more than twelve of
them " in the whole isle," but at one
time they had been much more nume-

rous. It has been conjectured that the *sloggorne* they recited were "fragments of Ossian"; but even learned St. Andrew's, where five were in the habit of convening in Martine's time, had scarce the training and accomplishment necessary for the appreciation of the wild cadenzas of a Celtic chant of battle; while as for the benighted Lowlands in general it is to be feared that if Celtic tarmagants with tag and tatter had there essayed to "roup and rook" in Ersch their Ossianic *sloggorne*, their only *largesse* would probably not have differed greatly from that with which Mahoun requited the "clatter" of the Highland contingent in the nether regions :—

> " The Devil sac deaved was with their yell
> That in the deepest pit of hell
> He smorit them with smook."

Is it an altogether unreasonable supposition that this periodical bardic confabulation at St. Andrew's bore some remote and traditional reference to the city as an

ancient and renowned seat of learning and
the arts? May not the custom have
originated in a sentiment of regard on the
part at least of some of the earlier among
these minstrels for their *alma mater?*
Possibly none of Martine's twelve—when
the mystery was decayed and moribund—
had any real tincture of college training;
but that some disciples of learning did not
disdain this method of getting their bread
may be concluded from the mention, in the
Act of 1578 for repressing vagrants and
minstrels, of "vagabond scholars of the
Universities of St. Andrew's, Glasgow, and
Aberdeen, who were not licensed to ask
alms by the Rector and Dean of Faculty."

Much of the earlier poetry of Scotland
was undoubtedly the work of beggar-bards.
Such an one was Blind Harry himself, who,
according to John Major, by reciting "in
the presence of men of the highest rank"
the verses which composed his "Book of
William Wallace" "procured, as he indeed
deserved, food and raiment." The earlier

Scottish kings, too, retained their peculiar poets; and Barbour records that in his day the border minstrel was a personage; so that it seems by no means improbable that to wandering minstrels—Miltons not mute but only inglorious—we are indebted for most of the matchless ballads tradition has preserved. True the bard is ostensibly treated with scant respect in the Act of 1457, being classed with sorners and feigned fools; but the key to the interpretation of this Act is to be found in another (1449), in which he is by implication excepted from punishment, only fools "who were not bards" being described as amenable. But after all some of the heroes of the ancient border ballads—as Cockburn of Hender-land, whose fate is bewailed in the "Lament of the Border Widow," and Johnnie Arm-strong of Gilnockie—were little better in the eye of the law than "sorners and masterful beggars"; and it seems beyond doubt that the border rievers, even if they did not keep their own special bards to beguile the

tedium of their idle hours, yet bestowed on
them substantial patronage and protection.
There is, however, clear evidence that even
at a later period the vocation of bard or
minstrel was not only deemed lawful, but
held in high esteem. An Act passed in
1471 granted them, with knights and
heralds, permission to be habited in silks ;
and more than a century after this (in
1574), while Highland or Irish bards or
beggars were prohibited from being received
in the Lowlands, minstrels, songsters, or
tale-bearers, in the service of a lord of
parliament, a great baron, or a burgh, were
specially excepted from the penalties
decreed against vagabonds. Yet this Act
probably indicates the beginning of the
end. General protection was practically
withdrawn from them, and above all the age
of chivalry was now no more. Individual
lords or barons might for a time retain
their own special minstrels, but the artless
art of the ancient balladist was lost
beyond revival.

X.

WHILE James I. of Scotland on the one hand took active and vigorous measures for the repression of sorning and every other form of mendicity on the part of all that were able to work for their living, on the other he introduced regulations which conferred on mendicity a repute to which it could not before pretend. True it is that from time immemorial pilgrims had been in the habit of living on the alms of the faithful, and that the Church, too, recognised an order of mendicant friars. But these cases were anomalous and peculiar: both friars and pilgrims chose the life upon religious grounds. That of beggar

students and candidates for the ministry
was not dissimilar, for these, too, had
chosen what was regarded as a high,
unworldly vocation, and to entertain them
as guests was generally regarded as an
honour and a privilege. But by the Act
of 1424 general mendicancy—only tolerated
till then—was recognised in the case of
qualified persons as a lawful and laudable
profession. Virtually the Act permitted
all not between the ages of fourteen and
seventy to beg in town and country; and,
moreover, it instituted, under the countenance and patronage of the local authorities,
an order of beggarhood for such as from
physical or mental defects were unable to
earn a living by any other means. Such
persons might be enrolled on application in
landward districts to the sheriffs and in
towns to the baillies. The most patent
and irrefragable qualification was blindness,
but the claims of lameness, if complete
enough, and of half-wittedness, if sufficiently decided, were readily acknowledged;

those who passed the test receiving a gaber-
lunzie, or beggar's badge, which conferred
the license to ask alms of all and sundry,
and the privilege of pursuing their calling
not only without molestation but with
every prospect of success. Possibly at
first comparatively few found it necessary
to take advantage of the Act, for in Edinburgh at least tokens do not appear to have
been issued to beggars till 1502, and then
only to prevent the increase of pestilence
by the influx of strangers. After the
Reformation the distribution of gaber-
lunzies was undertaken by the Kirk-sessions
which generally made it a *sine quâ non* that
the receiver should be a communicant;
and as by a clause in the Act of 1424 it
was charged that all non-licensed beggars
should work for their bread or be burned in
the cheek and banished the kingdom, the
result was that the Kirk not only invited
but compelled into her fold all "the halt
the lame and the blind."

In addition to the order thus established

throughout the kingdom, the king and
(probably in emulation of the royal example) many of the nobles extended
authority and countenance to a special
body of beggars called bedesmen. The
king's bedesmen were as many in number
as the king was years old; every Maundy
Thursday they assembled in his presence,
when their feet were washed by his own
royal hands, and they received a new
outfit for the year, including a blue gown,
a wooden cup and platter, a leathern purse,
as many pennies or shillings Scots as he
was years old, and a pewter badge with the
words "Pass and Repass"; they were the
aristocracy, the high dignitaries, of the craft;
their career, while much less toilsome and
anxious, was probably much more lucrative
than of most in the learned professions;
and no doubt the rank and file of beggar-
dom, recognising the honour and glory thus
shed upon their calling, regarded the pos-
sessors of its prizes with the mingled envy
and admiration customary in other profes-

sions. And as the calling, being thus
explicitly recognised as honourable, must
certainly have included many very worthy
and honest suppliants—many persons held
in general respect—the community seems
on its part to have co-operated with the
very spirit of the law, and to have minis-
tered to the needs of legalised mendicants
with ungrudging cordiality and cheerful-
ness. This may be inferred even from such
pieces of poetical satire as " The Gaber-
lunzie Man" and the "Jollie Beggar." The
" pauky auld carle " who " cam o'er the
lea" was ensconced in a comfortable " place
ayont the ingle," where he " cadgily ranted
and sang," and so thoroughly established
himself in the good graces of the daughter
of the house that she fled with him ere
morning; while the punctiliousness of the
Jollie Beggar in the selection of a bed-
room appears to indicate that a certain
choice as to quarters—humble though they
were—was both claimed and allowed.

The institution of a licensed order of

mendicancy seems to have been necessi-
tated by the Church's neglect of her duties
to the poor. In "The Dream" Sir David
Lindsay makes the misuse by the prelates
of the patrimony of Holy Kirk—

> " The third to be given to the poor is,
> But they dispersed that gear all other gatis
> On carts and dice, on harlotry and houris "—

one of the causes of their "punition" in
hell. Knox, too, wrote a satirical "Beggars
Summonds" to the friars to quit the "great
hospitalis," which properly belonged to the
poor. Dated "Fra the haill Cities, Towns,
and Villages of Scotland the Fyrst Day of
January, 1558," it was couched in the name
of "the Blynd, Cruked, Wedowis, Orphcil-
ings, and all other Pure, sa viscit Be the
Hand of God as may not worke."

At the Reformation the Kirk adopted
various measures of relief which tended to
decrease the necessity of begging; but, apart
from its gainfulness, the calling had the
recommendation of independence as well

as that peculiar charm which attaches to
adventure. By this time, too, the custom
had struck so deep that it could not be at
once eradicated. Not only so, but in spite
of the restrictions that hedged the calling
off, it was impossible to restrain the majority of those in difficulties from sharing in
its benefits. The severest enactments were
passed from time to time against unlicensed
mendicancy, but they were practically of
no avail. One permitted the detention of
strong and masterful beggars as slaves; by
another they could be seized and employed
in manufactories; a third constrained them
to toil in Government mines; provision was
made for their chastisement by the special
erection of correction houses; a stricter
supervision of the poor was enforced in
every parish; an endeavour was made to
contrive a better system of police. But
mendicancy went on flourishing more lustily
than ever, and shortly before the union
attained to proportions practically un-
manageable. After the union it began to

decay; but the professional beggar continued to ply his trade well into the present century, and the order of king's bedesmen was only abolished in 1833.

The national manna was the customary alms, and the "mealpowk" which figures in the poem of "The Jollie Beggar" remained the mumper's main equipment through the ages. Seldom did it happen, even when times were hardest, that he went empty away from the poorest door; and in the villages, so late as fifty or sixty years ago, it was still the householder's duty to minister to the blind beggar's needs, and pass him on from neighbour to neighbour until he had made the round of the place. He sold his meal to a dealer, and he was able to fare sumptuously in such haunts as "Poosie Nancie's" on the proceeds. In the country he was generally certain of a substantial supper in the farmer's kitchen and a comfortable bed of straw in the farmer's byre; and in many districts this tradition of hospitality lingers still. But the picturesque and venerable blue-gown, the carted cripple with his team of dogs, the half-witted ballad-singer in his faded fripperies—all these have long since gone their last rounds and passed from Scottish scenes. Perhaps their absence is no matter for regret; but has the problem of relief for the deserving poor been solved in such a way as makes the extinction of lawful beggary a theme for unmingled congratulation?

XI.

THE reason why the border riever was generally a Scot is chiefly geological: England
being a level country was easily robbed,
while southern Scotland, with its hills and
dales, its ravines and morasses, at once
rendered the work of spoiling difficult, and
afforded to the native riever good hiding
and safe shelter. In the palmy days of
freebooting the Borderer was an ideal robber.
Unsurpassed in daring and artifice he was
thoroughly respectable as well—as respectable and even pious as the border yeoman
of to-day. It was reputed of him that he
never said his prayers more fervently nor
told his beads with a more devout recur-

rence, than when his thoughts were also
turned towards a contemplated quest for
booty. Nor was the ardour of his devotions
in any degree affected by a secret consciousness of wrong-doing. He had no
such consciousness. He knew not of hy-
pocrisy. The intricacies of moral dialectics
were beyond his understanding. His code,
if not specially refined or exalted, was
neither subtle nor complicated, and he adhered to it with strict and conscientious
loyalty. He made no pretence of being
aught else than a riever. He knew of no
calling or profession to be esteemed so
highly; he could conceive no prouder ambition than to excel in it.

Originally he was rather warrior than
thief—his booty was spoil from an enemy.
Yet he was not an enthusiastic patriot. In
his heart of hearts he may well have cared
nothing for country and king. He had small
reason—he owed little to one or other.
When the Southron armies wrought havoc
in the Scottish dales he was left their first

prey; he received from country and king neither defence nor compensation. He had to rely on his own strategy and skill for safety and subsistence, so that he became a law unto himself and fought for his own hand. Except for the aid he was only too willing to render in the wars against England, the border chief claimed entire independence of action, and he even aspired to a certain joint sovereignty with the Scottish king. Thus the minstrel of Johnnie Armstrong :—

" When Johnnie cam before the king
  Wi' a' his men sae brave to see,
The king he movit his bonnet to him,
  He weened he was a king as weel as he."

Properly to gauge his character it must be recognised that circumstances made robbery compulsory—on other conditions or by other means it was impossible to live. " Since in time of war," wrote Bishop Leslie, " through invasion of enemies they are brought to extreme poverty; in time of

peace the ground, albeit fertile enough,
they utterly contemn to till, fearing that
shortly the wars oppress them. Wherefore
it comes to pass that they seek their meat
by stealing and rieving." In the beginning
their victims were chiefly the English; but,
the thieving habit once acquired, they soon
came to the conclusion that it mattered
comparatively little whether they thieved
from Southron or Scot. In a word, they
were Fabians with the courage of their
convictions: they were " persuaded that all
the goods of all men in time of necessity,
by the law of Nature, were common to
them and others." At the same time these
primitive Socialists were unfretted by that
blood thirst which (theoretically) charac-
terises so many propagandists of Socialism.
They abhorred the shedding of blood except
in time of actual war, and conceived that
not even for the necessities of life would
they be justified in the slaughter of Eng-
lishman or Scot. They had, therefore, to
substitute skill and sublety for force, and

they achieved such a perfection in the art
of thieving as has never perhaps been
paralleled. In their case, indeed, you have
a much more striking illustration of conscientious perseverance and its triumph over
adverse circumstances than any recorded in
the irreproachable books of Dr. Smiles. The
adaptation of means to ends was consummate. In its absolute simplicity of construction—its sagacious regard to essentials and
its rigid rejection of the superfluous—the
border peel was a veritable architectural
triumph. The aboriginal peel was wholly
of earth, and, being completely fireproof,
could be destroyed only at the cost of more
labour than the task was worth. Those of
stone—intended chiefly for defence—were a
later invention, the most of them being put
up in accordance with an Act of 1535, which
provided that they should be "threescore
futis of the square, ane eln thick, and six
elnes heicht." The primal peel was not
intended for defence, and was absolutely
unfurnished, nothing being left in it either

to take or to destroy. " If they but have
a swift horse," says Leslie of the peel-
dwellers, " and whereto they may dress
themselves and their wifes, they are not
meikle careful for the rest of the household
gear." Even the common domestic utensils
were a-wanting, the only piece resembling a
pot or pan being a " broad plate of metal "
used for baking the oaten cake. The riever
grew no vegetables, nor had he store of ale
or wine. His diet, alike at home and on
the march, was veritably Spartan. He
boiled his meat in the paunch of its original
wearer ; he baked the oaten cake, which
served for vegetables and bread alike, on
the " broad plate of metal " slung at his
saddle-bow; yet he cherished no disdain towards milk and cheese if they were on hand,
and for the nonce could dine contentedly
on sodden barley. It was chiefly this rigid
simplicity that made him invincible. He
laughed to scorn both Scots attempts
at repression and English endeavours at
revenge. When the need-fires warned him

of the coming of armed hosts he leapt into
the saddle, and with his children in front of
him and his wife at his stirrup made off to
the hills or to the woods. If the enemy
approached his lair he took to the moss,
and led him a wild-goose chase from which
he was lucky if he escaped with a ducking.
Unlike the Highlander, he was always a
rider. An absolute knowledge of every
peculiarity of hill and dale and stream far
and near was an essential accomplishment.
Having made his way unseen to the near
neighbourhood of a byre or field of cattle
he lay in hiding till dark, seized his booty
in the dead of night, and made off with it
along a line of retreat so adroitly contrived
that pursuit was well-nigh hopeless.

His moral standard was defective; but he
possessed in high perfection many noble and
manly qualities modern business methods
are not conspicuously successful in de-
veloping. In bodily hardihood he was
unsurpassed, and none could bear the
"stings and arrows of misfortune" with

a calmer or more constant heart. He had
also his own code of honour, which was
never broken. Unless in revenge of injury
he was guilty of no wanton wrong. To
family and kindred his devotion was un-
dying, and to all—friend or foe—his promise
was inviolate. It may be, too, that his
methods were not inherently more dis-
honest than many of those tricks of trade
the law winks at and the tame Briton
endures. What was best in his mode of
life is mirrored in the spirit, the fire, the
wild pathos of the ballads he inspired; and
most assuredly the generous and heroic
must have predominated over the mean
and selfish elements in a mode of life
which could inspire such genuine and
affecting strains.

XII.

THE original *rôles* of Saxon and Celt in
Scottish history cannot now be exactly
determined. The annals of these early
centuries are meagre, and perplex more
than they enlighten. At first the Celt
had probably the advantage of a superior
civilisation, but it was apparently incapable of expansion and development. His
romantic and rigid attachment to ancestral
habits made him unfit in the long run to
cope with the prosaic but practical Teuton.
How far he held his own in the Lowland
regions as regards the mere possession of
the soil is one of the puzzles of history;
but here at least his individuality, alike as

regards language, customs, and institutions
finally succumbed to the influence of alien
races. South and east of the Grampians
the Celtic civilisation became extinct; but
the wild and savage region behind—difficult
of access and presenting no temptation to
colonist or raider—remained the inviolate
home of a race which retained its purity
of descent and its primitive civility for
ages.

Scenery, climate, and the rigour of his
surroundings no doubt in the long run
stamped their impress on the character
and habits of the Celt as on his physical
frame; but if they affected his barbaric
peculiarities it was chiefly to accentuate
and confirm. In the world beyond his
mountains he had nor lot nor part. Dim
echoes of its movements, of its wars and
revolutions, may have reached his reclusion,
but they were soon forgotten as "a tale that
is told"; the seas brought him neither
braveries nor emasculating comforts; the
busy industries, the material wealth of the

Sassenach, he held in scorn ; his faint contact with the arts of modern civilisation
only caused him to cling more fondly to
his pristine usages. But his mode of life
had at least the merit of untainted simplicity. In diet, habit, and house he—as
Buchanan, Leslie, and Lindsay of Pitscottie testify—observed " the ancient par-
simony." True, in some districts the rule
of the nobles had partially broken up the
clan system when these authors wrote, but
even then there were regions under nominal
rule of the nobles where it flourished in as
full vitality as ever. Wild herbs eaten
raw, oatcakes baked on the immemorial
" Graedeal," game or fish cooked in savage
fashion in the ashes, were the customary diet.
In Commissioner Tucker's report in 1656
the district north and west of Dumbarton
Fyrth (the Firth of Clyde) is described as
still inhabited by the " Old Scotts or Wyld
Irish and speakeing theyr language, which
live by feeding cattle up and downe the
hills or else fishing and fowleing, and for-

merly, till that they have been of late restrayned" (by the energetic rule of Oliver), " by plaine downright robbing and stealeing." Over this wild region the Commissioner found the collecting of excise duties practically impossible. But in truth,. so far as liquor was concerned, the proceeds of the excise would have been insignificant enough. Unlike the Lowlander, the Celt was not a drinker of ale. His chief liquor was water from the running brook, milk being something of a luxury, while usquebagh was reserved chiefly for occasions of ceremony and rejoicing.

To eke out the supplies from his native hills the Highlander, as above recorded, had recourse to " creaghds," or cattle-raids. In the case of certain of the wilder clans cattle-raiding was in truth almost the only industry. Herein the fierce delights of feud or battle being intermitted, the warrior instinct of the cateran discovered a certain mild excitement. To spoil the Sassenach was also an unalloyed pleasure

in itself, and afforded some solace for the
loss of the Lowland straths and the fair
and fertile lands beyond Clyde and Tay.
But the habit of raiding did not contami-
nate or lower his general morality. Apart
from this inveterate eccentricity his
honesty, except perhaps in degenerate
modern times, was proof against well-nigh
any possible temptation. Of personal robbery he was incapable; and a stranger was
probably as safe from violence or wrong
in his domains as in a Quaker settlement.
The chief Sassenach movables which found
favour in his eyes were sheep and cattle;
but he limited his raiding to the latter. In
his code of honour the lifting of sheep was
a despicable crime; for sheep were held in
peculiar, in almost sacred, estimation on
account of their wool, and even in appro-
priating kine it was incumbent on him
strictly to observe the ancient methods.
The larceny was permissible only on the
order of the chief. And while lifting was a
noble and highly-respected vocation, the

cateran could not condescend to the mean-
ness of purloining merely one head of
cattle singly: this would have made him
kin to the common thief, and such kinship
he rejected with scorn. " Common tief !
common tief ! steal one cow, twa cow, dat
pe common tief! Lift hundred cow, dat
pe shentleman's drovers."

Like the Redskin brave, the cateran contemned all toil but that associated with war
or the chase ; he held in honour no craftsman save the maker of arms : all other
arts were appropriate to women or Sas-
senachs or slaves. Yet he could scarce
be charged with listlessness or sloth ; he
spared no pains to develop his muscular
strength and to acquire true cunning in
the use of his several weapons—bow, broad-
sword, dirk, and poleaxe. As he avoided
servile toil, his apparel and his domestic
arrangements were severely primitive. The
belted plaid, originally his only garment
(trews were an effeminate surrender to
climate) was practically a savage mode;

for the tailor was such an anomaly in old
Celtic life that the latter-day Highlander
could never allude to him but with stereotyped apology. And the plaid, as it was
the cateran's chief raiment by day, was
also his covering by night. His bed was
the heather, and even in wild weather the
sky was often his sole canopy. When the
stern colds of winter forced him to seek
the shelter of his turfs he arranged the
heather brush uppermost, so as to make
him a soft and warm couch. The hut,
with its beds of heather and its hearth in
the centre surrounded by circular stones,
was primarily the abode of wife, family,
and domestic animals; himself was accustomed to dine in the great hall of his
chief, and here he commonly spent his
evenings listening to the stories and songs
of the bard or sharing reels to the music
of the pipes.

The government of the clan was strictly
patriarchal, and to this must be ascribed
the strong and sacred character of the clan

sentiment. The bard (who was also the genealogist and historian) was held in peculiar honour. Originally, as in Ireland and Wales, he recited to the strains of the harp—in use in the Scottish Highlands as late as the sixteenth century. But gradually bard and harp succumbed to the bagpipes, proficiency whereon was held of such importance that special colleges were established for instruction in pipe-music under famous masters. Yet the bagpipe, it need scarce be said, is not exclusively a Celtic instrument. Possibly it may have been a legacy of the ancient Britons, and at any rate the suspension of its use in the Lowlands can be clearly traced to the interference of the Kirk-sessions on account of its association with dancing. In the Highlands its triumph over the harp appears to have indicated the decay of the clan sentiment. The tales and songs of the bard were of the past, and to the cateran the past had been much greater than the present was or the future could be. Dis-

guise it as he might, he was subject to
the Sassenach : the glories of his race
had vanished ; the old victories could be
no more. In all likelihood the recitals
were saddening rather than joyous in
effect ; and it may well be that the dance
was gradually preferred because it helped
the cateran to forget his griefs. At any
rate, while the harp is now mute in every
Highland hall the shrill music of the pipes
has gained rather than lost in power to
animate and enrapture the descendants of
the clansmen.

XIII.

THE Reformed Kirk of Scotland claimed the right to exercise absolute authority over conduct down to the minutest details. While it abolished the confessional, it none the less aspired to regulate not merely the outward acts, but even the inmost sentiments and beliefs of every member of the community. It assumed the entire moral charge of the nation individually and collectively; and the only possible means of escape from the rigours of its discipline was by the extreme expedient of committing a capital crime. " Blasphemy, adultery, murder, perjury, and other crimes capital worthy of death

131

ought not," says the First Book of Discipline, "properly to fall under censure of the Church," and this for the very sufficient reason that " all such open transgressors of God's laws ought to be taken away by the civil sword." The Kirk had done with them, and therefore required of the State that they should be " taken away." Every criminal—or rather sinner—who had not earned the right to be " taken away by the civil sword " was primarily answerable for his conduct to the Kirk authorities. The crimes specifically mentioned in the Book of Discipline as " properly appertaining to the Church of God to punish the same as God's Word commanded " were " drunkenness, excess (be it in apparel, or be it in eating or drinking), fornication, oppression of the poor, by exaction, deceiving of them in selling or buying by wrong weight or measures, wanton words, licentious living tending to slander." The list is pretty comprehensive, but it is rather illustrative than exhaustive. The Kirk had no com-

plete and definite criminal code, as regards
either specific acts or their punishment, the
distinguishing characteristic of her criminal
law being an extreme flexibility in the
direction of inclusiveness and severity.
Practically any act, whether public or
private, of any individual, whether gentle
or simple, became a crime if the Kirk-
session of his parish thought fit to make
it so. A similar flexibility also characterised her criminal procedure. Mere suspicion was frequently sufficient to place a
person under the ecclesiastical ban for
years, if not even for life. No strict laws
of evidence were adhered to, but almost
no method of obtaining evidence was too
despicable to be rejected. Gradually the
Kirk developed a system of espionage,
which while much more harassing than
the old confessional was quite as inquisi-
torial. Every form of transgression, no
matter how trivial, with every omission
of religious duty, was searched out by
elders and reported to the Kirk-sessions.

These detectives were told off to attend
fairs and races, and report on the conduct
of those who frequented them; and, like
the skeleton at the feast, their unbidden
presence damped the spirits of the most
jovial at every wedding and merrymaking.

None were permitted to claim exemption
from surveillance. " To discipline," decreed the inexorable Book, " must all the
estates within this realm be subject if they
offend, as well rulers as they that are
ruled." " The inviolable preservation of
God's religion," wrote Knox, in his *Exhortation to England*, " requireth two prin-
cipall thinges : the one, that power nor
libertie be permitted to any, of what estate,
degre, or autoritie that ever they be,
either to lyve without the yoke of discipline
by God's Worde commannded; either yet
to alter, to change, to disanull, or dissolve
the least one jott in religion, which from
God's mouthe thow hast receyved."
" And," he furthur adds, " as touching
execution of Discipline, that must be done

in everie citie and shire where the magistrates and ministers are joyned together, without any respect of persons; so that the ministers, albeit they lack the glorious titles of Lordes, and the develish pompe which before appeared in proude Prelates, yet must they be so stowte, and so bolde in God's cause, that yf the King himself wolde usurpe any other autoritie in God's religion, then becometh a membre of Christ's body, that first he be admonished according to God's Worde; and after yf he continue the same, be subject to the yoke of discipline." The special aim of the Kirk was to establish in England and in Scotland a theocracy modelled after that of the ancient Jews, with, however, this difference, besides others, that sacrifices and ceremonies were to be superseded by catechisms and confessions. The result was in Scotland—for England, notwithstanding Knox's prophetic warning that it would not "escape vengeance, which is already prepared for the inobedient," could

not be induced to make the experiment—
a wildly exaggerated travesty of a form of
government in itself entirely alien to the
genius of Europeans. The Kirk's authority
was deemed to be coextensive with the
nation. Her pretensions were quite as
arrogant as those of Rome, and they were
much more rigidly insisted on. To plead
non-membership of the Kirk, and decline
attendance on its ordinances, was simply
to incur its implacable attentions; and
should these prove ineffectual of repentance
and submission, forth came the dread edict
of excommunication. The obdurate re-
fractory was delivered over to Satan, not
in the merely formal fashion of to-day,
but in as literal and practical a sense as
mundane authority could achieve. He was
supposed to be actually given "into the
hands and power of the devil"; he was
declared to be "accursed," and "all that
favour the Lord Jesus" were required so
to "repute and hold him." The effect of
this was a system of "boycotting" so in-

defatigable and relentless that no choice was left but an unconditional surrender. If the impenitent were a servant no master might employ him. If he were a master no servant durst minister, on any pretence whatsoever, to his direst necessities; none might give him food, drink, or shelter; his nearest and dearest were debarred from offering him the offices of friendship or even showing him common courtesy; he became incapable of holding any form of property; his enemies might do with him as they listed without let or hindrance.

In Scotland excommunication was much more terrible than mere outlawry. Powerful nobles frequently defied the king with comparative impunity, but they could not so defy the Kirk. How prodigious was the force of her anathema, and how vain even for the strongest to contend against it, might be illustrated by many examples; but it may suffice to cite the cases of the first Marquis of Huntly, the ninth Earl

of Errol, and the fifth Earl of Bothwell,
all occurring during the rule of James VI.,
and at a time when the Kirk was by no
means at its meridian of power. Huntly,
a Catholic by conviction, to escape the
terrible results of excommunication, more
than once came under solemn covenant to
observe the ordinances of the Kirk and
even to communicate. Errol, less amenable to menace or persuasion, incurred in
1608 the penalty of £1,000 for absenting
himself from communion; was enjoined
to confine himself within the bounds of
the city of Perth for " the better resolution of his doubts "; and being ultimately
found " obstinate and obdured," was excommunicated, and laid in close durance
in Dumbarton Castle. As for Bothwell,
being long the special champion of the
Kirk, he was able with its countenance to
defy the displeasure of King James, but
having mortally offended the clergy he
came under the ban of excommunication,
and had not only to put a final term to

his alarums and incursions, but to depart
the country and to spend the closing years
of his life in penury and exile.

The secret of the Kirk's authority rested
in her prerogative of excommunication;
the curious blending of spiritual maledic-
tion with temporal tyranny in her anathema enabling her virtually to usurp the
authority of the kingdom. With such a
tremendous weapon in reserve, too, she
could afford to be comparatively lenient in
her other modes of enforcing obedience; but
the mildness of these subsidiary methods
was more apparent than real. Their seeming lenity was greatly qualified by comprehensiveness of application, and by the Kirk's
persistent importunity. Even attendance
on religious ordinances was made to assume
a disciplinary form, everything being ex-
cluded fitted to render the services attractive to the natural man. While also
regularity of attendance was imperative,
wakefulness during services, however prolonged, was enforced by a variety of devices

more ingenious than refined ; and this was
supplemented by periodical examination of
every citizen, whether communicant or not,
to test doctrinal soundness and progress
in religious and theological acquirements.
No assumption of dulness or stupidity
exempted from censure ; for while great
patience and forbearance were manifested
towards weak-minded devotees, such persons
as manifested any intelligence and ability
in the daily duties of life were handled
with the sternest severity if at all back-
ward in the acquirement of that knowledge and those convictions essential to fit
them to take their place as communicants.
" Everie maister of houshald," so was it
decreed in the Book, " must be commandit
eathir to instruct or ellis caus be in-
structed his children servandis and
familie in the principallis of the Christiane
religioun" [as understood by the Kirk].
And again : " Such as be ignorant in the
Articulis of thair Faith ; understand not,
nor can not rehearse the Commandimentis

of God; knaw not how to pray; neathir whairinto thair richtuousnes consistis, aught not to be admitted to the Lordis Tabill. And gif thay stuburnlie continew, and suffer thair children and servandis to continew in wilfull ignorance, the discipline of the Churche must proceide against them unto excommunicatioun; and than must the mater be referred to the Civill Magistrat. For seing that the just levith be his awin faith, and that Christ Jesus justifieth be knawledge off himself, *insufferable we judge it that men shall be permitted to leve* and continew in ignorance as members of the Churche of God." Thus the Kirk virtually menaced death against all who refused her yoke of intellectual and moral bondage. It must also be remembered— though this may appear something of an anticlimax—that at stated intervals, as well as on special occasions, there were enjoined on all alike such fasts as did actually and literally occasion the severest qualms; and that this torture was in-

geniously augmented by exposure to a prolonged series of exercises austerely diversi-
fied with exhortation and rebuke.

The system of public discipline introduced by the Kirk for actual transgression
was to some extent a revival of an old
Catholic custom which had fallen into
desuetude ; but it was characterised by the
same bald and bare austerity that distinguished the Presbyterian ceremonials.
Whatever be said of certain modes of
Catholic discipline there are few, if any,
that verge on the ridiculous, while there
are some (as that of pilgrimage) that are
touched with a certain beauty and romance.
By her contempt for ceremonial, her dread
of what she deemed to be idolatry, and her
rejection of art, the Scottish Kirk necessarily deprived herself of a powerful means
of kindling the imagination of her penitents.
Nearly all her modes of discipline were
informed with a certain grotesque and
awkward strain which tended to provoke
the laughter of far other than the mere

ribald. The small delinquencies were commonly visited with admonition, and the formal admonition of adults in a public assembly is apt to seem more or less childish and pedantic. But the chief disciplinary instrument was what Burns calls the "creepy chair." There were two varieties—a high and a low; promotion to the more conspicuous depending upon the flagrancy of the offence. The professed penitent remained on the stool all through divine service, the presence of the congregation at worship being supposed to lend solemnity and severity to the chastisement. Usually the offender was clad in a "harn gown" (the *San Benito* of the Presbyterian Inquisition), and various other signs of opprobrium might be attached at discretion. Thus the discomfort of special offenders was further enhanced by the application of the branks—a vile contrivance in iron plates, whose chief function was to serve as a gag; and in the case of males the head was sometimes shaved.

For minor trespasses—as scolding, quar-
relling, abstinence from church, violation
of the Sabbath, playing at cards, and so
forth—the usual punishment was confine-
ment in the joug, an iron collar attached
to the outer walls of the church. This
discipline was administered only on Sundays, but might be continued from week
to week in succession. A not uncommon
alternative was fining. Sometimes the
defaulter was held in bondage for long
periods in the kirk steeple; or the specially
obdurate might be banished the parish, or
delivered over to the magistrate to be
scourged or burned on the cheek. In
extreme cases ducking in pools notoriously
foul and rancid was also practised, some of
the more enterprising Kirk-sessions equip-
ping themselves with a special apparatus
for the purpose.

During Knox's supremacy the ideal system of Kirk authority expounded in "The
First Book of Discipline" was undoubtedly
in full sway. The principal members of the

nobility subscribed the book; the Privy
Council of Scotland gave it their sanction
previous to Mary's arrival from France; and
although the Queen herself naturally declined to ratify it, the absence of her impri-
matur rendered it no whit less operative.
The Regent Morton was the first to take a
decided stand against the clerical claim to
absolute rule, one of the main aims of his
policy being the subordination of Kirk to
State. As a flagrant instance of the
Regent's opposition to the execution of discipline, the Kirk historian, Calderwood, nar-
rates that " Robert Gourley, an elder of the
kirk of Edinburgh, was condemned to make
his public repentance in the kirk of Edinburgh upon Friday, the 28th May, for trans-
porting wheat out of the country. The
Regent being advertised, answered for him
when he was called upon to utter his con-
fession, and said openly to the minister, Mr.
James Lowsone, ' I have given him license,
and it pertaineth not to you to judge of that
matter.' " This example, of course, rather

illustrates the comprehensiveness of the
spiritual prerogative claimed by the Kirk
than the pretensions of Morton; but if all
tales be true, Morton once gave much more
startling evidence of the scant respect in
which he held her discipline, for he is said
to have actually caused one of her clergy to
be first tortured and then hanged for daring
to rebuke him for adultery. This was
taking the bull by the horns; for had the
charge of adultery been sustained, himself,
according to the "Book of Discipline," had
been liable to the extreme penalty of death.
But while as a private individual he had
incurred the Kirk's severest condemnation
in more ways than one, it was as a ruler
that he had contrived to give her especial
offence. He seriously crippled her pecuniary resources, and he studiously refrained
from carrying out her special behests.
Though "often required," says Calderwood,
"to give his presence to the assembly and
further the cause of God, he not only refused but threatened some of the more

zealous with hanging, alleging that otherwise there could be no peace or order in the
country." But in the end the Kirk was
victor; for it was chiefly owing to his rash
defiance of her that Morton was driven
from power and was visited by the doom
with which he had menaced her froward
representatives.

Under King James the Kirk was shorn of
much of her ascendancy, alike in matters
temporal and matters spiritual; but on one
important point of discipline the harmony
between Kirk and king was without jar or
discord. Both were equally exercised by
and alarmed at the extraordinary manifesta-
tions of Satanic enterprise revealed in the
presence of sorcery and witchcraft: James,
because personally he greatly dreaded the
application of witchcraft against himself;
the Kirk, because it discerned in it a special
attempt on the part of Satan to overthrow
its own dominion. Thus the chief result of
the interest aroused in the community by
the wonders recorded in the Jewish Scrip-

tures, joined with the indefatigable attention
the Kirk had seen fit to consecrate to the
politics of the nether world, had been a sort
of apotheosis of perhaps the most gruesome
and repulsive of all superstitions. Of its
astounding influence in depraving the popular imagination, the grave narrative of the
Kirk historian, Calderwood, supplies a characteristic example. "In the moneths of
November and December" [1590], "manie
witches were taikin : Richard Grahame,
Johne Sibbet, *alias* Cunninghame, Annie
Sampsone, middlewife, Jonet Duncan in
Edinburgh, Eufame Makcalzeane, daughter
to umquhile Mr. Thomas Makalzean, Bar-
bara Naper, spous to Archibald Dowglas of
Pergill, Jonet Drummond, a Hieland wife,
Katherine Wallace. They conspired the
overthrow of the king and queen's fleete,
at their returne out of Denmarke, by raising
of stormes upon the seas. Sindrie of the
witches confessed they had sindrie times
companie with the devill, at the kirk of
Northberwick, where he appeared to them

in the likenesse of a man with a redde cappe, and a rumpe at his taill, [and] made a harangue in maner of a sermoun to them; his text ' Manie goe to the mercat, but all buy not.' He found fault with sindrie that had not done their part in ill. Those that had been bussie in their craft, he said, were his beloved, and promised they sould want nothing they needed. Playing to them upon a trumpe,* he said, ' Cummer goe yee before; cummer goe yee,' and so they daunced. When they had done, he caused everie one, to the number of threescore, kisse his buttocks. Johne Gordoun, *alias* called Graymeale, stood behind the doore, to eshew, yitt it behoved him also to kisse at last. John Feane, schoolemaister of Saltprestoun, confessed he was clerk to their assemblies." Thus it would seem that the weird conventions of the wicked were closely modelled after the assemblies of the Kirk down even to the preparation of an autho-ritative record of their desperate purposes

Jew's-harp.

and pactions. The craze had indeed achieved
a rankness of growth and a virulence of
habit without parallel in the world's history ;
and the zeal displayed by the king in
seconding the Kirk in her attempt to sup-
press the traffic with Satan and shield the
prey of Satan's minions from calamity, went
far to reconcile her to his lukewarm support
in other fields of activity.

The breach between the Kirk and king
did not become irreparable till the time of
Charles I. The policy of Charles can scarce
be defended, but it is at least as defensible
as the policy of the Kirk. His aims were
not one whit more tyrannical than hers ;
intrinsically they were less so, for they had
to do merely with " tithes of mint and anise
and cumin," while she concerned herself
chiefly with the " weightier matters of the
law." If the king endeavoured to interfere
unduly with her forms and ceremonies, her
persistent ambition was to subdue both king
and people to her authority. Thus she
would have the covenant not only tolerated

but subscribed by the king ; and in the hey-
day of her supremacy she endeavoured to
impose it on England as well as Scotland.
In a sense her design was frustrated by
Cromwell even in respect of Scotland; but
although that great and masterful ruler debarred her from direct and active interference with the civil arm he permitted her
while he reigned the exercise of almost un-
limited control over manners and morals.
The session and the presbytery records, in
every district of the country, during the time
of the Protectorate, teem with astounding
instances of her interference with even the
minutest details of domestic and social life.
Elders were appointed each in his own
quarter for trying the manners of the
people; and the Presbytery of Aberdeen
went so far as to order every master of a
house to provide himself with a " palmar,"
or birch, for the chastisement of frivolity in
his family or among his maids.

It is impossible to arrive at any other
conclusion than that the ancient disciplinary

system of the Kirk was a huge and dreadful mistake; that while her enforcement of it was the usurpation of functions properly belonging to the State, her manner of exercising these functions was insufferably tyrannical. Granted that she had to contend with a certain laxity of manners created by a peculiar religious crisis, the cures she prescribed were in effect little better than the disease. If her ideal was noble—and it was so only in the sense in which the monastic ideal is noble, for it represented but an incomplete and bastard monasticism—her methods were intolerable. Small wonder, then, that at the Restoration she should have been hoist with her own petard. The Covenanting persecution, cruel though it was, was not unprovoked, nor did it essentially differ from the Kirk's own method of behaviour towards heretics. Moreover, its victims were possibly not so numerous as those immolated by the Kirk on the altar of witchcraft. Much has been made of the pitiful fate of the two Cove-

nanting women exposed to drowning by the
gradual influx of the waters of the Solway;
but the odium attaching to this isolated act
is slight indeed compared with that pertain-
ing to the torturing, " wirrying," and burning, at the direct instance of the Kirk, of
whole multitudes of women, many of whom
died protesting in all sincerity that they
were wholly " innocent of the crimes laid to
their charge," and none of whom could have
been actually guilty in the sense supposed.
Besides, the Covenanters did not object to
religious persecution on principle, but only
as exercised against themselves. They knew
nothing of toleration. With a free hand
they would have concussed both nations
into Presbyterian Calvinism; and now an
attempt was made to concuss them into
Episcopacy. It was inexpedient and wrong,
no doubt, and it proved a complete failure.
But it at least taught the Kirk the salutary
lesson that two could play her game of
religious tyranny; and from the furnace a
large part of the nation came forth wiser if

sadder than when it went in. The old pretensions of the Kirk were never revived in
all their pristine intemperance and self-
sufficiency. From henceforth she ceased
from exercising absolute sway in matters
civil; and in 1690 her old form of discipline
was knocked on the head by the repeal of
"all Acts enjoining civil pains upon sentences of excommunication." With this
tremendous weapon all but innocuous in
her grasp, she gradually discovered that her
subsidiary methods of punishment were
coming to be regarded with other than the
old emotions. The sanction of custom
enabled her to retain them in position for
some considerable time; but they had lost
much of their impressiveness. In this there
was hardly matter for regret on any account;
for her discipline, however unpleasant and
discomforting, had never been strikingly
effectual—indeed, could pretend to a victory
in connection with but a single sort of
transgressions. It was claimed that witchcraft did actually succumb to the vigilance

of the Kirk-sessions, and when in 1743
further persecution of witches was forbidden
by the civil authority, the Kirk protested
against such enlightened legislation as
" contrary to the express law of God; by
which a holy God may be provoked to permit Satan to tempt and seduce others to
the same wicked and dangerous snares."
But in truth witchcraft was chiefly a ghost
of the Kirk's own raising, and the cruelties
exercised in laying it form, perhaps, the
darkest blot on her escutcheon. It was
far otherwise with her efforts to cope with
the vice of drunkenness, the increase in
which may be partly explained by a desire
to find a refuge from the gloomy dogmatism
of the Kirk and the joyless social atmo-
sphere of Puritanism. It was also far other
with her championship of the seventh com-
mandment. As for the " cutty stool " as a
moral influence, " A frail victim," says Hill
Burton, " was sometimes compelled to ap
pear on nine or ten successive Sundays
exposed to the congregation in the seat of

shame "; but "the most noticeable effect
often produced by the exhibition was in the
gibes and indecorous talk of the young
peasants, who, after a few significant glances
during the admonition, and a few words at
the church door, adjourned the general
question for discussion in the change-
house."

Within recent years the competition
between the various denominations has
tended in the direction of moderation. In
any case, the more formidable paraphernalia
of punishment have nearly if not utterly disappeared. The joug still hangs by the outer
wall of Duddingston Kirk—it may be as a
warning to the youth of adjacent Edinburgh
against Sunday skating on the neighbouring loch; but not within recent years have
news been brought to the Scottish capital of
any actual application of the discipline. The
stool of repentance has also ceased to vary
the monotony of Presbyterian ceremonial
and—a Samson shorn and captive—may
now be contemplated without peculiar per-

turbation in antiquarian museums. No
fetid ecclesiastical pool now reminds the
philosophic traveller that "justice shall
haunt" the loose-tongued woman as well as
the "violent man." After years of degenerate and spurious observance, the Fast Day
is now avowedly consecrated to recreation
and frivolity. As to the services, even in
those sections of the Kirk which specially
claim to represent "the distinctive principles of the Reformation," it is now almost
recognised that the proper means of ecclesiastical influence is not compulsion and
mortification but persuasion and charm.

XIV.

In the fifteenth and sixteenth centuries—
to go no further back—the importance
attached in Scotland to richness and elegance of attire is abundantly shown, not
only by portraits but by allusions in the
poetry of the period and by a great variety
of documentary evidence. Thus, of the
successful merchant in "The Priests of
Peebles"—

> " Rich were his gowns, with other garments gay,
> For Sunday silk, for ilk * day green and gray ;
> His wife was comely clad in scarlet red."

There is, indeed, every probability that

* Every.

the Scots, in the centuries preceding the
Reformation, were more attentive to dress
than the English. "They are," says the
Spanish Ambassador, at the Court of James
IV., of the Scots ladies, "very graceful and
handsome women. They dress much better
than here" [England], and "especially as
regards the head-dress, which is, I think,
the handsomest in the world." Again, of the
young nobles and barons : "There is much
emulation among them as to who shall be
best equipped, and they are very ostenta-
tious." Even when he did not enlist in
foreign service, the young Scots gentleman
usually spent some years in foreign travel—
especially in France, Spain, and Italy—and
his manners were, in great part, modelled
after those of the gayer south. Moreover,
Scotland had then a wide and good commercial intercourse, and imported large
quantities of silks and other braveries.
Even of the country damsels, who danced
"full gay" at "Christis Kirk on the
Green," you read that "their shune were

of the Straits." Nor must the French
influence at the Court of Mary of Guise,
and her daughter, Mary Stuart, be left out
of account. "Sour John Knox" refers
disdainfully to the "stinkin pride of
the women," at the opening of Mary's
Parliament in 1563, and states that
articles were in this "Parliament presented for order to be taken for apparel,
and for reformation of other enormities,"
but that all was "scripped at." But from
a letter to his sisters it would appear that
his own private opinion in regard to female
adornment was not thus Puritanical and
grim. Although he "cannot approve," he
declines absolutely to condemn "sic vain
apparell as maist commonlie now is usit
among women"; he thought it "difficult
and dangerous to appoint any certainty."
The "Monstrous Regiment of women"
(female government), gave him real concern; but in respect of dress he was
disposed to make allowance for natural
vanity and unreasonableness; he deemed

it at least better that they should feed their
minds upon the trifles of the toilet than
meddle with politics and "public authority." He rallied the ladies of Mary's
Court on their love of finery with gentle
mockery ; he did not directly reprove. " O
fair ladies," said he, " how pleasing were
this life of yours if it should ever abide,
and then in the end we might pass to
heaven with all this gay gear ! " The Act
of 1567 regarding ladies' apparel—" This
Act is verray guid "—was somewhat mild :
" Item it be lauchfull to na women to weir
abone hair estait except^e howris." This
peculiar conjunction of " let " and " hindrance " is a curious illustration of Scots
pawkiness. No penalty is prescribed. It is
merely announced that to dress above their
station is a privilege henceforth reserved to
" unfortunate persons." It was not that
the legislators loved prostitution more ; it
was that they wanted to impale the
devotees of personal adornment on the
horns of a bad dilemma.

11

According to " The First Book of Discipline," " excess in apparel" was one of
the faults which " properly appertained to
the Church of God to punish "; and although there seems to have been much
liberty at first, yet gradually every kind
of personal adornment came to be regarded
as more or less of " a snare." In 1575 an
Act was passed by the General Assembly
of the Kirk anent " the apparelling of the
ministers." The Reformed clergy had
rejected the dress of the Catholic priest-
hood with the " disguised apparels " of the
several religious orders. They adopted
civil dress ; and the regulation shows how
very ornamental and elaborate it was, and
what difficulty the Kirk authorities had in
subduing the love of the beautiful and
becoming in the " preachers of the Word."
" Forasmuche," the Act proceeded " as a
comelie and decent apparrell is requisite
in all, namelie ministers, and such as beare
function in the Kirk, first, we thinke all
kinde of browdering unseemlie ; all begaires

(slashes) of velvet in gowne, hose, or coat, and all superfluous and vaine cutting out, steeking with silkes, all kinde of costlie sewing on pasments, or sumptuous and large steeking with silkes; all kinde of costlie sewing or variant hewes in clothing, as reid, blew, yellow, and such like, which declare the lightnesse of the minde; all wearing of rings, bracelets, buttons of silver, gold or other mettall; all kinde of super-fluities of cloath in making of hose; all using of plaids in the Kirk by readers or ministers; all kinde of gowning, cutting, doubletting, or breekes of velvet, satine, taffatie or such like; and costlie giltings of whingers and knives and such like; all silk hatts, and hatts of diverse and light colours; but that their whole habite be of grave colour, as blacke, russet, sad gray, sad browne; or searges, worsett, chamlett, grogram, lylis worset, or such like; that the good Word of God, by them and their immoderateness, be not slandered. And the wives of the ministers to be subject to

the same." Although this order primarily
affected the ministers and their families
alone, it necessarily influenced powerfully
the whole community. "Sad gray" and
"sad brown" were now authoritatively recognised to best befit the godly, and
"variant hues," as red, blue, yellow, and
such-like, were declared to be more or less
akin to wickedness. Moreover, since the
clergy avowedly adopted civil dress, they
no doubt set the fashion among the
middle classes, at least in the case of
those who desired to be of pious repute.

In its efforts to discountenance gay
apparel the Kirk was greatly aided by
Parliamentary legislation. In 1581 an Act
was passed against "the great abuse among
the common people, even of the meanest
rank, in their presuming to counterfeit the
King and the nobility by their habit of
wearing costly clothing of silk." This
was renewed in 1584, and subsequent enactments indicate the difficulty of breaking
down the natural instinct. Sir Richard

Maitland's "Satire on the Toun Ladies" supplies evidence to the same effect :—

> " Thair gouns ar coistlie, and trimlie traillis,
> Barrit with velvous, sleif, nck and taillis ;
> And thair foirskirt of silkis seir
> Of fynest camroche thair fuksaillis ;
> And all for newfangilnes of geir.
>
> And of fyne silk thair furrit cloikis
> With hingand sleivis, lyk gcill poikis ;
> Na preiching will gar thame forbeir,
> To weir all thing that sinne provoikis ;
> And all for newfangilnes of geir."

It was one of the special foibles of James VI. to prescribe appropriate dresses for the different classes and functionaries. The dresses now worn by Scottish officials—including judges, advocates, and magistrates —date from an Act passed in 1610, and were personally determined by the King ; and this enactment was supplemented by one of 1621 for the regulation of civil attire. None but nobles were permitted to wear gold or silver lacing, nor any velvet, satin, or silks. Lords of session, barons, magistrates, professors at Universities and others were permitted to indulge

in a style of adornment something less
gaudy; but all other persons were prohibited from having pearls or lacings upon
their ruffles, shirts, napkins, or socks; as
also from wearing "buskings of feathers,"
pearls or precious stones. "Austere and
Puritan self-denial in dress" was thus
rendered compulsory as regards the most.
It was lauded by the Kirk as a special
token of grace, and the attitude of the
Kirk was supported by legislation reserving
ornament to them that were favoured of
the King, if not of Heaven. And by this
general prohibition of ornamentation the
standard of taste was lowered, until the
nobles themselves lapsed into the adoption
of the sad and sombre style of the middle
classes. No doubt other influences—as
the decay of feudalism and chivalry—were
working towards the same end. Nor did
the case of Scotland essentially differ from
that of other countries; only the authority of
Puritanism was there more rampant, and to
some extent antedated the period of change.

XV.

At one time there was probably very little to choose between Scots and English in the matter of filthiness and general insanitation. In all verity the fastidious sensibilities of the scornful Howell—who published in 1639 his "Perfect Description of the People and Country of Scotland "— seem to have been grievously shocked by their experience of so "stinking a town as Edinburgh "; but not so long before the southern capital might fairly have vied with Edinburgh in potency and variety of odour. It is certain, indeed, that even in the palmy times of her uncleanliness the latter city never boasted such an artery of putrefaction as the Fleet River, whose effluvia did so clog the neighbouring airs

as to assimilate the incense burnt at the
adjacent altars. In Howell's time (and
chiefly under the auspices of King James,
born, as he states, "in stinking Edinburgh ")
a good deal had been done for the sanita-
tion of London by the construction of main
sewers; but not more than three years
before the publication of Howell's satire on
the Scots—and in simple deference to the
plague of 1636—had the noisome Fleet been
bridged and covered in; and for more than
a century after—as is sufficiently attested
by her astounding bills of mortality, London
remained a whited sepulchre. But besides
endeavouring to cleanse the outside of the
cup and platter, she gave abundant evidence of a desire to effect a remedy, however unable from lack of practical skill to
do so. Now, Edina (" Scotia's darling
seat "), so far from manifesting any anxiety
to be rid of her stenches, became seemingly
only more fondly attached to them as time
went by; and by the middle of the seventeenth century her advance in cleanliness

had only been an advance backwards. Her magistrates bore a bad repute for their scandalous neglect of her amenities. More than a century before Howell and his "Perfect Description," Dunbar, in his "Address to the Merchants of Edinburgh," had inveighed in no measured terms against the hideous and universal squalor of her streets. Of London he had sung thus :—

" Gemme of all joy, jasper of jocunditie
   Most myghty carbuncle of vertue and valour,
Strong Troy in vigour and in strenuytie
   Of royall cities rose and geraflour,
   Empresse of townes, exalt in honour,
In beawtie beryng the crone imperiall,
   Swete paradise precelling in pleasure
Londoun, thow art the floure of cities all."

But this is how he pictures his native capital :—

" Tailors, soutters, and craftis vile
   The fairest of your streets does file,
   And merchants at the stinkand style,
     Are hampered in ane honey came ;
     Think ye not shame
   That ye have neither wit nor will
    To win yourself a better name."

And even if his rebukes did for a moment
pierce the hides of municipal self-com-
placency and sloth, it is probable that with
the other achievements of his robust and
admirable muse they passed into oblivion
at the Reformation, and at any rate they
failed to produce any lasting salutary effect.
To such a hideous pass were matters
presently come that in March, 1619, the
Scottish Privy Council found it necessary
to represent to the magistrates that "the
city is now become so filthy and unclean,
the streets, the vennels, the wynds, and
the closes thereof so overlaid and covered
with middings and with the filth of man
and beast, as that the noble councillors,
servants, and others of his Majesty's subjects who are lodged in the burgh cannot
have clean or clear passage and entry to
their lodgings"; and they further give
them candidly to know that "this shameful and beastly filthiness is most detestable
and odious in the sight of strangers, who,
beholding the same, are constrained with

reason to give out many disagreeable
speeches against this burgh, calling it a
puddle of filth and uncleanness the like
of which is not to be seen in any part of
the world." So that Howell was not by
any means the first to indulge in "dis-
graceful speeches" against the birthplace
of King James. Nor, if the condition of
Edinburgh was even half as vile as it is
painted in this Act of the Scottish Privy
Council, is there any reason to deprecate
his satire. Indeed there is evidence even
to excess that the Scottish capital, as well
as other Scottish burghs, maintained an
equal disregard of the amenities beyond
the close of the seventeenth century.
Even after much amendment had taken
place as regards the removal of middens
and other permanent centres of putrefaction, it was very slowly and painfully that
her citizens, notwithstanding the repeated
interference of authority, were weaned from
the immemorial custom of paying their
nightly orisons to the divinities of the

midden by discharging the daily accumu-
lations of filth from their windows into the
streets.

Without doubt this peculiar reluctance
of the Scot—even him of the "modern
Athens"—to part with his ancient habit
of uncleanliness is traceable in no small
degree to the special bent of his religion
at the Reformation. It was said from of
old that cleanliness is next to godliness;
but if Scottish Puritanism be the highest
possible form of godliness on earth, then
cleanliness and godliness were incompatible
for centuries. That rage of iconoclasm
which was a special note in Scottish
Reformation zeal was in great part composed of a frenzy against beauty and art.
Cleanliness, if not promotive of godliness,
is certainly necessary to the realisation of
beauty, so that the Scottish reformer was
almost necessarily prepossessed in its dis-
favour. At least squalor and dirt were
thoroughly antagonistic to adornment and
"formosity." Possibly the very fact that

they were disagreeable was reckoned rather
a recommendation than not. That they
entailed any evil consequences, whether physical or moral, was opposed to the general
tenor of Knox's teaching and the teaching
of Knox's disciples. Nay, the pest which
had scourged the land for centuries they
were so far from regarding as a result of her
shameless uncleanliness, that they especially
described it as God's judgment upon sins of
an entirely different character, and Knox
himself assumed the right to prophesy it
upon the enemies of the Kirk as one of his
peculiar prerogatives. The endeavours of
the secular power to induce the adoption of
cleanlier habits in the towns and burghs
were frequent enough ; but, comprehensive
as was the authority claimed by the Kirk
over manners and morals, she never indicated the smallest discontent with the
national vice of squalor. In the secular
statute-book of Scotland there is at least
one Act (1424) against the wearing of
" ragged clothes " ; but, while " excess in

apparel" is specially designated in "The
First Book of Discipline" as one of the
sins which "do properly appertain to the
Church of God to punish the same as God's
Word commandeth," a significant silence
is maintained as to unkemptness and un-
washedness, and even as to deficiency in
clothing. It is even possible that the
assemblage of a whole congregation in
"harn gowns" would have rejoiced the
preacher as a peculiar token of the opera-
tion of grace, for personal adornment was
persistently discouraged by the Kirk. So
that, however great may be the debt of
Scotland to Knox, and however beneficial
to her may in some respects have been his
influence, it is to be feared that by the
guidance alone of him or his disciples she
would never have obtained deliverance from
the slough of her uncleanliness.

XVI.

THE writer on football in the ninth edition of the *Encyclopædia Britannica* affirms that, "unlike cricket, football had never taken root among the aristocracy and gentry." This may be true of England from the time of Edward III.'s prohibition, but as regards Scotland it is altogether the reverse of true, and probably for this reason —that the royal fiat there was never very potent. Each individual noble was a law unto himself, and the Scottish kings were by no means successful in substituting archery for football and golf. Football was prohibited in 1424, 1451, 1471, and 1491; but the very repetition of the enactments is

proof of their inefficiency. At all events
in 1497 footballs were purchased by James
IV. himself, probably for a game at Court.
In the next century the game was played
not merely by the gentry, but even by the
monks and other ecclesiastics. Thus Sir
David Lindsay's abbot vindicates his Pres-
byterial efficiency by setting his prowess at
football against his neglect of the pulpit :—

> " I wot there is nocht ane among you all
> More finelie can play at the fut-ball."

Even the highest nobles did not disdain
the game. Of the " Bonnie Earl of Moray "
the balladist sings :—

> " He was a braw gallant
>   And he played at the ba' ;
> And the bonnie Earl of Moray
>   Was the flower among them a'."

Another noble who " played at the ba' "
was the fifth Earl of Huntly, who was
seized with apoplexy (it was hereditary)

while kicking off, and died the same night.
The game seems to have been a common
one at the Court of Queen Mary. Sir
Francis Knollys tells that when she was
at Carlisle after the flight from Langside,
" about twenty of her retinue played at
football before her the space of two hours,
very strongly, nimbly, and skilfully, without
any foul play offered." Their play struck
Sir Francis as much superior to anything
he had seen; and it is clear that the game
in vogue at this time among the upper
classes of Scotland differed radically from
the common annual rough-and-tumble of
later years. True, James VI., in the
" Basilikon Doron," published in 1599, de-
nounces the pastime as " meeter for laming
than making able the users thereof," but
the modern forms of the game have been
decried in similar terms.

The real cause of the decline and dete-
rioration of football in Scotland was the
prohibition of Sunday football by the Reformers. The traveller William Lithgow,

in his poem " Scotland's Welcome to King
Charles," 1633, laments that—

> " Manly exercise is shrewdly gone,
> Football and wrestling, throwing of the stone ;
> Jumping and breathing, practices of strength
> Which taught them to endure hard things at
> length."

During the Covenanting and Cromwellian
periods of ascendancy football was in still
greater disrepute ; and Sir David Hume of
Crossrig records that, in 1659, having, in
accordance with a traditional custom of the
second-year students at Edinburgh University, taken part in a game of football on
the Borough Muir on the 11th of March, he
was sentenced to be whipped in the class,
and, refusing to submit, was expelled the
University.

Some have supposed that the ancient
pastime in Scotland allowed running with
the ball, as in the modern Rugby game, and
in support of this Hone's account of the
" historical game at Scone " has been

quoted. This game, however, as is stated in the original notice in Sinclair's " Statistical Account " of the parish, was only a carrying game, the use of the foot not being lawful ; moreover, according to tradition, it was not of English origin, but was introduced into Scotland by an Italian in the days of chivalry; above all, it was notoriously peculiar to Scone, and hence the current proverb, " All is fair at the ball of Scone." There is no evidence at all that carrying was permitted in the pure Scottish variety. Thus, in Skinner's " Monymusk Christmas Ba'ing "—

> " Sometimes the ba' a yirdlins ran,
> Sometimes in air was fleeing " ;

but although the Monymuskers are represented as employing " a' the tricks of fut and hand," there is no allusion to any one running even a " yirdlins " with the ball in his arms, for that was only " fair " at Scone. But is the Scone game not practically identical with the Greek and Roman with the

harpastum? Here, then, we seem to have
a key to the origin of modern Rugby. If at
Scone, the presumption is that the Roman
game was played in other parts of Britain ;
and Rugby football seems to be nothing
more or less than a combination of the
Saxon and Roman games, with a supple-
mentary " scrum " derived from the period
when football, having been under a ban in
England from the time of Edward III., had
degenerated into " a friendly kind of fighte,"
engaged in once a year by an unskilled mob,
not infrequently in the narrow area of the
public streets.

In all probability the ancient game of
football in Scotland bore a close resem-
blance to the modern Association game,
except that holding with the hand was
allowed in certain emergencies. It may
have been quite as scientific, for constant
practice at any game necessarily leads to
the substitution of skill for mere brute
force. Skilled players would hardly care to
take part in a game played with one hundred

men or upwards a side, as in the border game of Sir Walter Scott's time, and we have seen that only about twenty players took part in the game before Queen Mary. No doubt " accidents " at the game are still more numerous than is desirable, but the immense improvement—in the supersession of savagery by skill—which has followed the general adoption of the game by all classes of the community is undeniable. Those who, by a long parade of " accidents," attempt to frown the pastime down as brutal and demoralising are merely doing their little best to make it both. And, after all, is it as now played exceptionally dangerous? Minor accidents are common enough; but, so far as loss of life is concerned, is football as perilous as hunting, shooting, riding, yachting, bathing, or even doing nothing? Is it very much more deadly than crossing a crowded London street? or is it anything like so hazardous as railway travelling?

XVII.

No tenet nor practice, no influence nor power nor principality in the Scotland of the past has outvied assassination in ascendency or in moment. Not theoretically, indeed, but practically, it occupied for centuries a distinct, almost a supreme, place in her political constitution—was, in fact, the understood if not recognised expedient always in reserve should other milder or more hallowed methods fail of accomplishing the desired political or, it might be, religious consummation. To trace its rise from opprobrium to honour, or fully to account for its predominance in Scottish politics were perhaps a somewhat arduous task. Yet is it easy to discern some of the principal causes of its influence. The turn

for it is in the Celtic blood, of which there
was a strong infusion even in the Lowland
Scot ; while there can be little doubt that
the limited nature of the king's prerogative,
combined with the rivalries between the
almost monarchical nobles, secured it a
certain immunity from punishment, and
also prepared a soil specially fitted for its
development. The respect for law and
order was of very slow growth. For centuries such justice as was exercised was
haphazard and rude, and practically there
was no law but the will of the stronger.
Few, if any, of the great families but had
their special feud ; and feuds once originated
survived for ages : to forget them would
have been treason to the dead, and wild
purposes of revenge were handed down from
generation to generation as a sacred legacy.
To take an enemy at a disadvantage was
not deemed mean and contemptible, but—

> "Of all the arts in which the wise excel
> Nature's chief masterpiece."

To do it boldly and adroitly was to win a

peculiar halo of renown; and thus assassination ceased to be the weapon of the avowed
desperado, and came to be wielded unblush-
ingly not only by so-called " men of honour,"
but by the so-called religious as well. A
noble did not scruple to use it against his
king, and the king himself felt no dishonour
in resorting to it against a dangerous noble.
James I. was hacked to death in the night
by Sir Robert Graham; and James II. rid
himself of the imperious and intriguing
Douglas by suddenly stabbing him while
within his own royal palace under protection of a safe conduct.

The leaders of the Reformation discerned
in assassination (that of their enemies) the
special " work and judgment of God." The
martyr Wishart, described by Knox as " of
such graces as before him were never heard
within this realm," and by his pupil, Tylney,
as " courteous, lowly, lovely," was more
probably than his cousin the Wishart who
(in 1544) was an intermediary between
Henry VIII. and certain Scots conspirators

in a plot against the life of Cardinal Beaton;
and when the assassination did take place
in 1546, all the savage details of it were
set down by Knox with unbridled gusto.
"These things we wreat mearlie," is his own
ingenuous comment on his performance.
The burden of George Buchanan's "De
Jure Regni apud Scotos" is the lawfulness
or righteousness of the removal—by assassination or any other fitting or convenient
means — of incompetent kings, whether
heinously wicked and tyrannical or merely
unwise and weak of purpose; and he cites,
as a case in point and an "example in time
coming," the murder of James III., which,
if it were only on account of the assassin's
hideous travesty of the last offices of the
Church, would deserve to be held in unique
and everlasting detestation.

The bands or covenants of the nobles to
support each other in all their enterprises
(for their own aggrandisement) generally
implied a sanction of assassination if all
else should fail; and a place once gained

for it even by implication, it not infrequently
assumed the place of honour, till bands were
formed avowedly for the bare and sole purpose of assassination, when its position as
an influential factor in Scottish politics was
assured. The sanction or arrangement of
any particular murder by a nobles' league
was a very sure guarantee of safety for the
assassin ; and, as matter of fact, in the
great political assassinations of Scotland
immunity from capital punishment has
been the rule. Also they became so
numerous that in all probability the
national destiny has been more powerfully
and permanently affected by them than by
battles : always excepting, of course, the
battles of the early times and of the struggle
for independence. At least this was so in
the sixteenth century, which, after all, is
by far the most pregnant in Scots history.
Would the Reformation in Scotland have
come when it did, or would it have come
at all, or when it did come would its form
have been so radical and extreme had not

the purposes and schemes of Cardinal Beaton been brought to nought by his removal? The most striking circumstance of the murder of Riccio was the contrast between the Italian's physical contemptibility and crouching terror and the abounding energy and tumultuous wrath of his assailants; but politically considered, its far-reaching results can scarce be exaggerated. It saved the lives or fortunes of the most powerful of the Protestant nobles; it broke the power of the queen; it prevented the establishment of Catholicism; and it was the prelude of one of the strangest dramas in history, for its direct and almost inevitable consequence was the tragedy at Kirk-o'-Field. Darnley was disqualified, intellectually and morally, from being aught but a political shuttlecock; but the effects of his assassination sealed the destiny both of Catholicism in Scotland and of Queen Mary. Excepting Knox, the next victim, the Regent Moray, was perhaps in Scotland the most powerful personality of

his time. His removal failed of the direct
and special consequences anticipated, but
there can be little doubt that it greatly
affected the tenor of events. It came at
a critical period of his career; a few years
longer and the final aims of his ambition,
good or bad, wise or unwise, must have declared themselves; and his character, with
its strangely contrasting features, would
have been less of an enigma than it is.

These four murders have a peerless pre-
eminence; but the old influence may be
traced in Scottish history to a much later
period. The haunting terror of assassination was largely responsible for many of the
eccentricities, moral and political, of the
" Scottish Solomon "; and not till the
union of the crowns did the practice begin
to show decided symptoms of being on the
wane. To trace its indirect results is of
course impossible; but among them may
be reckoned the solemn leagues and covenants, which might never have been thought
of but for the old assassination bands.

XVIII.

PERHAPS of the paradoxical in politics no more curious example could be found than the great, almost pre-eminent, part played by Darnley in the events of his time. His one gift, so to say, was the result of a peculiar combination of weakness and baseness. Had he been cleverer or greater villain his career had perhaps been less momentous. It was the inordinateness of his moral debility rather than of his positive wickedness that made him such an efficient marplot of the schemes both of Mary and her opponents. To the assassins of Riccio he proved a dupe and tool of matchless suitability for their particular purpose; and yet Mary found in him an equally admirable

accomplice in robbing them of the main
fruits of their daring venture. His joint
capacity for dupery and treachery was
so inordinately rank that it counted for
one of the potent political forces of the
period, and in no small degree assisted in
constituting the few short months which
comprehended the assassination of Riccio
and his own tragic death one of the epochs
of Scottish history. But fruitful of great
results as had been the unrestrained action
of his imbecility, these were more than
matched by the consequences which followed
his "taking off"; for his death proved to
be the turning-point in the final struggle
between Catholicism and Protestantism in
Great Britain, and has up till now remained
the centre of one of the most burning of
historical controversies.

From the time of his marriage to the
Queen of Scots Darnley was almost fore-
doomed to calamity, if not assassination.
The career of any one who became Mary's
husband was bound to be eventful, but in

the case of one with Darnley's peculiar idiosyncrasies it was necessarily fated to be
short. The causes that made for his assassination thickened with amazing rapidity.
Originally danger threatened him only from
the Protestants, including Moray, who, it
has been argued, had already set his ambition on the Scottish throne; or from the
Hamiltons, who had rival claims with
Darnley to the Scottish throne apart from
his marriage to the Queen of Scots; or
from nobles such as Argyll, who had an
hereditary feud with his family. With the
murder of Riccio and escape of Mary the
dangers so increased that his fate was
practically sealed. What might have been
the result had Mary not won him over to
flee with her to Dunbar it is difficult to
forecast. Possibly her escape did little to
effect ultimate events, except as they bore
on her reputation with posterity. Had she
not escaped she might have been saved
from entanglement in Darnley's assassination, and her reputation with posterity

as Catholic martyr might have been un-
dimmed. As for Darnley, all that can
be said is that practically he left nothing
undone that could compass his own death.
First and foremost he had, as M. Philippson, in his "Histoire du Règne de Marie
Stuart," * points out, won for himself the
hatred, " implacable and mortal," of his
consort Mary Stuart; for besides having
been party to the murder of her most
trusted political confidant he had burst her
conspiracy for a Catholic conquest of Great
Britain : he had done so unconsciously
indeed, but in such a manner as to render
wedlock to him an intolerable encumbrance.
As regards the Protestants, he had shown
that in the character of avowed friend and
ally he was much more dangerous than as
open foe. Even nobles such as Morton,
who, though Protestants were " devoted to
him by bond of blood," he had hopelessly
estranged by a wanton betrayal of their
interests ; and diplomatists like Maitland

* Vol. iii. Paris, 1892.

he had outwitted and ruined by the incal-
culable peculiarities of his moral idiocy.
To crown all there was the rise to a position of supreme influence in the councils
of the queen of the sinister Bothwell, whose
one, but all-sufficient, objection to Darnley
was that he stood in the way of his ambition. Such in outline were the influences
which worked together to effect Darnley's
death. The chief question of historians
has been as to the character of their combination—as to which were principal and
which subordinate.

M. Philippson, in his recent volume, has
propounded the notion that the main contrivers of the Darnley murder were the
leaders of the Protestant nobility, with apparently the connivance of Cecil ; and has
assigned as their main motive that "they
saw in him as Catholic prince a dangerous
adversary, not on account of his personal
qualities but of his position as husband of
the queen and father of the future king of
Great Britain." The credibility of this

conclusion would have been more apparent
had Darnley not at this time been notoriously and hopelessly estranged from the
queen. On account of the estrangement
he had already become and seemed destined
to remain a political cypher, and therefore
so far as Protestantism was concerned his
removal from the political arena was at this
particular juncture by no means urgent.
Indeed it might even be plausibly con-
tended that to the Protestants there was
meanwhile considerable advantage in allow-
ing Darnley to remain as husband of the
queen. To prolong the quarrel between
them rather than to bring it to a close
would probably have been the more prudent
policy. Hampered as both then were they
were practically powerless to effect much
harm to Protestantism. Bishop Leslie
would have had no scruple in ascribing
the assassination to mere Protestant zeal
had there been the semblance of a reason
for doing so; but in the short narrative
included in Mr. Forbes-Leith's " Narratives

of Scottish Catholics" (1885) he affirms
that it was done at the instance of Morton,
Ruthven, Lindsay, and other assassins of
Riccio, and solely in revenge for the betrayal of their plans to the queen. This is
of course a by no means correct account of
the origin of the conspiracy, and indeed so
far as both Morton and Lindsay are concerned it is palpably the reverse of true, for
Morton declined to take part in the assassination, and Lindsay, who also, like Morton,
was a relative of Darnley, knew nothing of
it—as even Lord Herries admitted—and
cherished the deepest resentment towards
the supposed murderers. But the bishop's
theory manifests at least his disbelief in the
plausibility of such a theory as that of M.
Philippson, whose curious speculation indicates a strangely erroneous conception of
the individual idiosyncrasies of the Scottish
nobles. Even had Darnley been at this
time the main anxiety of the Protestant
nobility a divorce would have served their
purpose quite as well as assassination; and

thus Bishop Leslie clearly saw that if they were to be saddled with the responsibility of the assassination, revenge, and revenge alone, must be assigned as the motive. But plainly the main concern of the Protestant nobility at this time was to strengthen their position by obtaining the recall of Morton and other exiled assassins of Riccio. The assent of Bothwell and the queen to their recall indicates that if the leaders of the Protestant nobility did favour the assassination of Darnley they did so for the special benefit of Bothwell if not also of the queen. With their recall there arose the danger that the scale of political influence might be turned against Bothwell and the queen, and it would never have been agreed to except on the clear understanding of a *quid pro quo.* That *quid pro quo* was undoubtedly riddance from Darnley with a view to the queen's marriage to Bothwell. It is admitted that the leaders of the Protestant nobility did agree to a divorce; and the idea of assassination must

have been suggested by considerations more
urgent or more vehement than any that
primarily concerned Protestantism. M.
Philippson has himself unconsciously guided
his readers to these considerations, and has
thus supplied the best possible refutation of
his own theory, by proving that as early as
the Craigmillar conference Bothwell and
Mary had determined in one way or other
to be rid of Darnley. Mary, as he conclusively shows, was passionately attached to
Bothwell. The attachment may—as some
deem it necessary to suggest—have had its
origin in gratitude; for it was to him that
she chiefly owed recovery of her crown and
kingdom after the murder of Riccio; but
the theory that Mary throughout acted
from semi-compulsion or self-interest, while
it worsens rather than betters her case, is
entirely opposed to the whole tenor of the
evidence. Moreover, one of the main arguments against the possibility of Mary's
attachment to Bothwell—that he was desti-
tute of personal attractiveness—can scarcely

longer be persisted in. It never had much
cogency—hardly more indeed than the
theory that she was the victim of Bothwell's sorcery—but in any case it seems to
be now entirely refuted, not merely by the
statement of the Venetian ambassador
("Calendar of Venetian State Papers")
that he was "a young man of handsome
presence," but by the significant testimony
of even Bishop Leslie himself ("Narratives
of Scottish Catholics"), that he was "en-
dowed with great bodily strength and mas-
culine beauty." But be this as it may,
that Mary had already determined to marry
him "in spite of the whole world," is manifest from the fact that immediately after
the Craigmillar conference she began to
adopt measures to secure his divorce from
Lady Jean Gordon. It is thus abundantly
evident that at the time of Darnley's assassination riddance from him was a matter of
more vital moment to Bothwell and to Mary
than to any one else.

That Maitland was accessory to the

murder of Darnley—if he did not suggest
it or the arrangements for it—is more than
probable, for his close confabulations with
Bothwell at this particular time can scarce
be explained otherwise; but although he
had very good reasons for detesting Darnley
—supposing Darnley were worth more than
mere contempt—he was never supremely
devoted to Protestantism, at least in its
Scottish form. He had, in fact, long
ceased to enjoy the confidence of the
Presbyterians; for some time he had in
addition to this been on a very doubtful
footing with Moray; and by his marriage
to the beautiful Mary Fleming he was
linking his fortunes more closely with those
of the queen. His main difficulty no doubt
was Bothwell, who, in addition to his
personal unfitness to occupy the great
position to which he aspired, was his
bitter enemy; but he had no choice meanwhile except submission to Bothwell's ascendancy, and he may also have believed in
the possibility of ultimately frustrating his

ambition to obtain the queen's hand. As
to Moray, it is impossible to suppose him
entirely ignorant of the conspiracy, although
perhaps he purposely avoided acquaintance
with its methods and details. Apart altogether from Mary's account of the Craigmillar conference signed by Huntly and
Argyll, and inadmissible as evidence in
itself, the chances are that Moray was
perfectly well aware that Darnley's assassination had been purposed. One who had
attained to a position of such prominence
and authority among the Protestant nobility, and whose fortunes were at this time
in so critical a condition, was bound, even
for his own safety, to adopt every pre-
caution to obtain reliable information regarding such an important move on the
political chess-board. Besides, the conspirators had been by no means reticent
as to their intentions. That " something
bad " was contemplated against Darnley
had even reached the Spanish ambassador
in London. But Moray's opponents—what-

ever rumours may have been put into circu-
lation by them—did not directly charge him
with anything worse than neutrality : the
resolution to avoid entangling himself either
in endeavours to save Darnley or in plans
for his murder. Possibly he may have
deemed it best meanwhile to maintain an
attitude of masterly inactivity, and allow
Bothwell and the queen full freedom to
accomplish their own ignominy ; but there
were other manifest reasons to prevent his
interference. Apart from the fact that he
had no interest in saving Darnley's life, he
had also to look to his own safety. Bothwell would have welcomed any excuse for
getting rid of him as well as Darnley.
Indeed his chief danger at this time was
not from Darnley, but Bothwell. He had
done his best to ruin Bothwell, and he
could not suppose that Bothwell had forgotten it. From Bothwell he could expect
nothing more than mere sufferance. That
he was influenced in permitting the assassination by considerations of immediate ad-

vantage, beyond those of mere personal
safety, is, however, out of the question.
As matter of fact, the success of the plot
brought to him meanwhile not merely political extinction, but a great worldly disaster,
for Huntly's support of it—as well as consent to Bothwell's divorce from his sister,
Lady Jean Gordon—had been purchased
by promise of restoration to his forfeited
estates then held by Moray. That promise
—while it indicates how deeply the queen
was involved in Bothwell's machinations—
is sufficient proof of the small influence
which Moray then exercised in the councils
of either. Possibly could Moray have saved
Darnley's life without endangering his own,
he might have interfered (there is nothing
to show whether he would or not), but even
had he desired to perform an act, in that
ruthless age, of such exceptional chivalry,
he would probably like Morton—who from
motives of kinship, not chivalry, may have
desired to save Darnley—have been pre-
cluded from interference by his knowledge

of Darnley's almost phenomenal weakness
of character. This was of itself sufficient to
frustrate all efforts to save him. Of his
manner of welcoming interference on his
behalf, Lord Robert Stewart had unpleasant experience. It entirely coincided
with Morton's estimation of Darnley, that
he " was sic a bairne that there was nae-
thing tauld him but he would reveal it to
the queen again." At Kirk-o-Field Lord
Robert ventured to convey to Darnley an
intimation of his danger, and for his pains
was confronted with the queen, when in
dread of his life he deemed it best to deny
having uttered words bearing any resem-
blance to those reported to her by Darnley.
The fact was that Darnley was his own
worst enemy. Friendship with him had
become not merely an impossibility but
a positive danger; and all that can be
charged against Moray or Morton is that
they avoided an effort to save him, which,
while it would probably have been ineffectual of its purpose, might have proved

fatal to themselves. While, therefore, there
is no reason to suppose that had the Protestant nobility apprehended deadly peril
to themselves or to Protestantism from
Darnley, they would have scrupled even to
assassinate him, they could not have been
influenced by such a motive at this particular time. Protestantism had nothing
to do with the murder except indirectly.
Some of the Protestant nobles, from motives
of private interest or considerations of personal safety, were its abettors; others of
them were probably quite content that he
"sould be put off by ane way or other "—
by assassination if not by divorce, provided
they were not involved in the crime; but
its main contrivers—leaving Mary meanwhile out of account—were those who
"took the deed in hand ": Bothwell, who
of all the conspirators had immeasurably
the most pressing reasons for getting rid of
Darnley; Huntly, who of all others was the
noble most closely leagued with Bothwell,
and who was influenced solely by hope of

restoration to his forfeited estates; Sir
James Balfour, the provider of the lodging
at Kirk-o-Field, who was then a close parti-
san of Bothwell, and quite ready to sell his
services for any form of lucre ; Argyll, who,
although Protestant of Protestants, had
from the beginning been one of the most
strenuous opposers of the queen's marriage
to Darnley, with whose father his rival
neighbour, the Earl of Lennox, he had a
hereditary feud ; and the Hamiltons, who
as near heirs to the Scottish throne, were
personally the most bitter foes of Darnley
and his father, and were prepared to
welcome almost any conspiracy that increased the chances of their own succession. All these as well as Maitland—
who had very good reasons for cherishing
a strong personal grudge against Darnley,
and was at the same time anxious to in-
gratiate himself with the queen—remained
the allies of the queen after her marriage
to Bothwell. Probably to each and all of
them the marriage was detestable, and in

their allegiance to her, they were therefore
influenced either by loyalty to her person,
or by dread of the possible consequences of
their crime.

The main difficulty of the question is as
to the part played by Mary. Was she confederate ? or how far was she confederate ?
Was she one of the main authors of the conspiracy? Did she approve of it ? Did she
consent to it ? Was she an agent in it ?
Was she a mere dupe and tool ? or was she
entirely ignorant of it ? That she was in
entire ignorance that Darnley's death had
been determined on has ceased to be maintained except by her more fantastical devotees. Yet is the position of such artless
visionaries less hazy and inconsistent, if
more aloof from contact with reality, than
the faltering and paltering pleas of her more
subtle apologists. Mary, it is admitted, did
induce Darnley—her champions or apologists affirm from excess of innocent simplicity—to take up his residence in the
lodging at Kirk-o-Field, which the assassins

designed to be his shambles. Her chief
motive for choosing the half-ruinous and
isolated dwelling was avowedly a tender
regard for his health, which it was supposed
might have been injuriously affected by the
mists and damps that clung round Holyrood; but yet it would appear that after
the assassination neither resentment nor
horror at the discovery of the base purposes
for which she had been utilised, lessened in
the smallest her esteem and affection for
the chief assassin. Even M. Philippson—
who cannot, however, exculpate Mary from
responsibility for the murder, the more
especially as he admits her passionate devotion to Bothwell—has fallen a prey to
a form of this seductive yet suicidal reason-
ing. While admitting that Mary knew that
the assassination was in contemplation—
and so far from desiring to prevent it, was
quite willing to accept it as a preliminary
to her marriage to Bothwell, the chief
assassin—he has the courage to ask his
readers to disbelieve that she designedly

placed Darnley in the power of his enemies,
and actually arrives at the conclusion that
Darnley was taken to Kirk-o-Field at his
own request. Granted that it was so, the
casuistry of the plea is too refined for
modern appreciation ; but the hypothesis,
inherently incredible in itself, is without
tangible evidence to support it. For his
remarkable deduction he adduces no better
reason than the statement of Nelson,
Darnley's page, that Darnley was taken
to Kirk-o-Field because he declined to go
to Craigmillar. But Nelson did not say
that the ruinous and isolated lodging at
Kirk-o-Field was Darnley's special choice;
nor would it have mattered anything if he
had said it, for it is notorious that Darnley
had nothing to do with its selection. Moreover the statement of Thomas Crawford—
the retainer and friend of Darnley—which
is also appealed to in support of the same
conclusion, is to the effect that Darnley
was willing to go with her wherever she
might take him, even supposing she de-

signed to cut his throat; and that Crawford, who suspected some evil design, advised Darnley that he should stipulate to be taken to his own house, apparently Holyrood, and certainly not Kirk-o-Field, about which Darnley knew nothing whatever until his arrival in Edinburgh.

But the main difficulty of those who seek to absolve Mary from the charge of direct or indirect agency in the murder, is to discover a plausible reason for her sudden desire for Darnley's companionship, especially in view of the arrangements she had already made for her marriage to Bothwell. If she still contemplated marriage to Bothwell, the society of Darnley must in the circumstances have been specially distasteful to her. Unquestionably she would never have chosen it except from sheer necessity. M. Philippson suggests that she wished to frustrate an absurd scheme of Darnley for seizing the government, but can it be seriously maintained that this gave her the smallest anxiety?

14

Could the menace to her authority at this particular time from the pitiful intrigues of Darnley have been deemed more than infinitesimal? Moreover, if serious and immediate danger was apprehended from him there was only the more clamant call for his assassination; and does the explanation therefore not tend to strengthen rather than weaken the supposition that by enticing him from Glasgow she intended to facilitate the designs of the assassins? She knew that such designs were contemplated, and undoubtedly they would rid her of all danger from Darnley's intrigues. Why, therefore, trouble about these intrigues, if the assassins had determined on his death, and if they had resolved to effect it without her aid?

The only other possible supposition is that she wished to make a last effort to patch up a reconciliation with him; but this, as M. Philippson at once recognises, is quite untenable. She was already too irrevocably committed to Bothwell to

dream of going back, and even if thoughts
of compunction and pity had moved her to
a last effort at reconciliation she could
scarce suppose that a reconciliation could
be safely effected with Bothwell looking on.
But, besides, we have not been left to mere
conjectures as to the extent to which she
might have indulged in such inconsistent
and witless vagaries. A glimpse has been
afforded us by De Silva, the Spanish ambassador, of her real attitude at this time
towards Darnley, and it completely disposes
of the question of reconciliation. After
Darnley's arrival at Kirk-o-Field, Morette,
or Moretta, the ambassador of the Duke of
Savoy, had, according to De Silva (the
quotation is from the " Calendar of Spanish
State Papers," 1892), " asked the Queen of
Scotland whether he should see the King
[Darnley]. She told him he would not,
and she did not think he would be pleased
to see him in consequence of the secretary's
[Riccio's] murder, he, the secretary, having
been a servant of Morette. The latter knew

that the King wished to see him, in order to
give him two horses for the Duke, and the
King had even told the Queen that he
wished to see him, whereupon she had re-
plied that Morette had declined to meet
him by reason of the secretary's death."
This curious example of Mary's diplomatic
finesse reveals how fresh and vivid was still
her memory of the part played by Darnley
in Riccio's murder, and how deep, heartfelt,
and incurable was her alienation from him.
Well might Dé Silva infer from Morette's
" mode of speech " that Morette " was not
favourably disposed towards the Queen "
as regards her connection with Darnley's
assassination.

Further evidence of Mary's attitude towards Darnley is of course afforded by the
letters said to have been discovered in the
silver casket; and with the additional testimony to their genuineness made available
by the publication of the " Calendar of
Spanish State Papers " relating to this
period of Scottish and English history, it

seems impossible any longer to adduce even
a plausible pretence for excluding them as
evidence. In the comparatively mild language of the editor of the " Calendar," the
result of this new testimony is that the
" many arguments against their genuineness
founded upon the long delay in their production disappear." The language is mild,
for the arguments were founded chiefly on
suppositions and assertions ; and there was
in fact no evidence of long delay in their
production. But at any rate this additional
testimony deprives such arguments of their
last semblance of plausibility. We now
know that the French ambassador was
actually furnished with a copy of the letters
some time before the 12th of July, 1567, or
within three weeks after the time when the
casket was declared to have fallen into the
hands of Morton. The mere fact that the
French ambassador was officially furnished
with a copy of the letters that he might
show them to the French Court, is in itself
sufficient to remove any possible shadow of

doubt as to the truth of Morton's declaration that the letters were "sichted," or officially examined; and the argument that the letters are "under suspicion" from the mere fact that the casket and its contents remained "for eighteen months in the hands of Morton" becomes still more devoid of cogency. The supposed difficulties as to the language in which the letters were written are also completely disposed of. The ambassador must have obtained a copy of the original French version of the letters. The sending of a Scots version of the more important passages of the letters to Elizabeth—surely not on the face of it an unaccountable procedure if it be remembered that Scots was the native language of Scotland, and that in all probability also these were the very identical passages that were read to the Scottish Parliament in justification of the action against the queen—has been made much of by certain critics; but however ingenious or forcible such arguments may have seemed in the past, it can

henceforth avail little to ask why the letters
were sent to Elizabeth in Scots ?   The procedure may have been stupid or even inex-
plicable—as some, to whom one would wil-
lingly defer, seem to think ; but henceforth
it will be impossible to argue that it implied
deceit or criminality.   Another point also
is—as the editor of the " Calendar " points
out—" that the French ambassador in London knew the purport of the letters early in
July at a time when it was impossible for
Moray to have been informed of their existence."   Clearly, therefore, the supposition
that Moray, when at the end of July he
gave a description of the long Glasgow
letter, was then simply engaged in the process of forging it, and had not yet decided
on the precise form it should assume, is no
longer tenable.   But more decisive than all
is the consideration that it is no longer
possible to suggest that any portion of this
letter has been borrowed from the declaration of Darnley's retainer, Thomas Crawford.
The correspondence between the two docu-

ments, however it may have occurred, can
no longer be adduced as an argument that
the letter was forged on the basis of Crawford's statement. If the one document has
been based on the other, the only possible
conclusion now is that Crawford "refreshed
his recollection by aid of the letter." Thus
the main difficulty to the acceptance of the
Glasgow letter as genuine disappears. It
was really the only plausible evidence ever
adduced to support the theory that the
letters were forged or " doctored." Latterly
the theory that they were forged throughout
has, for more reasons than can here be
stated, been abandoned, but the theory that
they were doctored is in itself much more
incredible. " Doctoring " is of course a
suggestive epithet, but to practise " doctoring " of documents is, if not more difficult,
more dangerous than to forge throughout.
Indeed, as usually promulgated, the theory
was almost hopelessly involved in contra-
dictions ; for what advantage could be
gained by doctoring writings of Mary that

were already compromising? And if they were not compromising what was there to prevent Mary exposing the doctoring process?

The chief value of the long Glasgow letter is not that it more conclusively establishes Mary's connection with the murder—for apart from it the circumstantial evidence is overwhelming—but that it more clearly reveals her motives in consenting to act as confederate of Bothwell, and contains her best available apology or defence. The mitigating circumstances of the case are there stated more persuasively than by those who have deceived themselves by the flattering unction that Mary's cause is served by the rejection of the letter. It discovers to us that the real author of the conspiracy was not Mary but Bothwell; that in all probability Mary, as indicated in her version of the Craigmillar conference, was originally strongly opposed to the murder, and that she was to a considerable extent the victim of Bothwell's overmastering purpose. Deeply and irreparably as Darnley had wronged her, hateful as was the very thought of reunion to him, she declared that for her "own particular revenge" she would have been no party to the murder. Even as it was the despicable part she had to play—more than pity for Darnley—caused her the keenest anguish. "I will never rejoice," so she wrote, "to deceive any one that trusts me" [Would a forger have been at the pains to reveal this noble trait of character?]; "yet notwithstanding ye may command me in all things"; and again, "Now seeing to obey you, my dear love, I spare neither honour, conscience, hazard nor greatness whatsoever" [How closely the sentiment of this accords with another declaration of hers recorded by Kirkcaldy of Grange as to her readiness to follow Bothwell to the world's end!]; "take it, I pray you, in good part, and not after the interpretation of your false good brother, to whom I pray you give no credit against the most faithful lover that ever you had or

shall have." But while passionate love to
Bothwell seems to have been what chiefly
reconciled her to her odious task, there was
also the overwhelming influence of other
circumstances to incite and nerve her to its
performance. Not only had Darnley by the
rankness of his offence incurred her un-
quenchable hostility, but he had become an
object of general hatred and contempt; he
was now virtually a political pariah, and
murderer as well as traitor, he had fully
earned his death. Moreover, regard must
be had to the genius and temper of the
time. The wild justice of revenge had still
a recognised place in the moral code of the
Scottish noble, and the Darnley murder
was only rendered possible by the laxity of
prevailing opinion as to the sacredness of
human life. Mary succumbed to that
laxity of opinion in circumstances of peculiar difficulty and temptation, and while not
the less was she responsible for the murder,
it is impossible to believe that in their
hearts any of those—except the Catholics

and Darnley's kinsmen—who afterwards took the most pronounced part against her, appreciably regretted his death. For us the chief abiding interest of the crime is in the light flashed by it on the schemes and intrigues of the rude and fierce society of the Scottish Court. It affords a vivid apocalypse of the passions, hates, and unscrupulous ambitions that mingled with nobler influences in effecting the triumph of Protestantism in Scotland.

XIX.

His office had a hoarier antiquity than that
of kingship itself; he represented chieftaincy
in almost its most antique form. Indeed if
chieftaincy underwent a change after the
break up of the larger tribes, the probability
is that it was a change towards the earlier
and simpler form. Also the attempt at
feudalism was successful within but a very
limited area of the Highlands, and even here
the success was more apparent than real.
The two systems could never properly com-
mingle, for chieftaincy was independent
of material considerations. Besides, most
clansmen were simply hunters, or herds, or
raiders, as their forefathers had been from

time immemorial. Their circumstances and
surroundings seemed to defy change. Of the
arts of civilised life they, less than two centuries ago, knew practically nothing. Their
social system pointed backwards to primeval
ages. To them the past alone was great;
the future could be great only in so far as it
resembled the past. The reverence with
which the chief was regarded was neither
official nor personal in the usual sense.
The clansman honoured the dead more than
the living, and the common ancestor above
all his descendants. The chief was the representative of this common ancestor, and
of an uninterrupted succession of ancestral
chiefs whose achievements in war and whose
prowess in the chase were the perpetual
theme of the bardic songs and recitations
which formed the true litany of the clan.
The consideration which determined succession was nearness of relationship to the
common ancestor. Hence the brother of
the reigning chief was preferred to the son
in the case of mental and physical fitness;

the elder son by concubinage or handfast
marriage to the son of priestly marriage.
Failing brothers or sons, the choice was
limited to the *Geilfine*, or relations to the
fifth degree. The successor was recognised
during the chief's lifetime. That an inter-
loper should usurp the office was almost
beyond the bounds of possibility, for it was
guarded as with a wall of fire, by sacred
tradition ; and that it could not be degraded
by one unworthy or unfit was guaranteed by
a privilege of veto vested in the elders of
the clan. No young chieftain who had
failed in the test of valour—generally the
leadership of some desperate raid—was permitted to rank in the succession ; and if,
after attaining the dignity, he approved
himself incompetent or tyrannical, he might
be summarily removed.

The goodliness of the chieftain's heritage
was truly remarkable. Does any worthier
or more genuine sphere for ambition now
exist ? Probably no human being ever
cherished a profounder sense of personal

dignity—undoubtedly a most important aid
to happiness. Though rude might be his
dwelling and squalid his surroundings, no
monarch ever received such noble homage.
" The ordinary Highlanders," wrote Burt,
" esteem it the most sublime degree of
virtue to love their chief," for indeed " he is
their idol ; and as they profess to know no
king but him (I was going further), so
will they say they ought to do whatever he
commands without inquiry." In such circumstances the chief's duties, if he was
worthy to fulfil them, could not fail to be
pleasant and humanising. For the most
part, also, he was untroubled of serious
care, for his feuds with his neighbours and
his raids on the Sassenach did but afford
him a zest of excitement more exhilarating
than that obtainable from the safer pleasures of the chase. As a rule, he had
neither poverty nor riches, and his ambition was limited to providing for the necessities of his clan (the complete conquest of
a neighbour was a very rare occurrence).

The small inconveniences incident to his ignorance of the modern amenities were undergone with unruffled stoicism; they were merely external and superficial. From a long line of ancestors inured to hardship and despising every form of excess, he inherited such a constitution as was almost a guarantee of perfect health; and when at last he went to join their company, the coronach sung by the women over his grave betokened eulogy and triumph even more than regret. The clansman's thoughts were concentrated as much on the dead as on the living; and by a more influential canonisation than that of the saints, the chief continued to live in the "songs, the conversation, the dreams and meditations" of succeeding generations.

The clan system of government was in its way an ideally perfect one—probably the only perfect one that has ever existed. Perhaps it was the very thoroughness of its adaptation to early needs

that made it so hard to adjust to new
necessities. In its principles and motives
it was essentially opposed to the bent
of modern influences. Its appeal was
to sentiment rather than to law or even
reason : it was a system not of the letter
but of the spirit. The clansman was not
the subject—a term implying some sort of
conquest—but the kinsman of his chief.
The chief had no title to indicate " a distant superiority." He was simply the
Macleod or Macpherson or Macshimei.
But while the clansman cherished a keen
sense of independence, and expected to be
treated by his chief with friendly famili-
arity, the cold and degrading equality typi-
fied in the Parisian citizenship—child and
parent of revolutions—would have had for
him no charm. It was his peculiar pride to
claim the relationship to a superior ; and in
itself the very thought of kinship was thus
inspiring and ennobling. Obedience became rather a privilege than a task, and no
possible bribery or menace could shake his

fidelity. Towards the Sassenach or the members of clans at feud with him he might act meanly, treacherously, and cruelly without check and without compunction, for there he recognised no moral obligations whatever. But as a clansman to his clan he was courteous, truthful, virtuous, benevolent, with notions of honour as punctilious as those of the ancient knight. Not only was the standard of public morality a high one, but it was impossible to evade or defy it. Most clans had a certain number of helots (descendants of captives), but pauper or criminal class there was none, for the crimes of the clansmen were committed only against his enemies, and it was by stealing from them that he relieved the stress of poverty. No code of laws—after all it may be a symptom of decay, and no proof of advance in the art of government— stood between him and the personality of his chief; and the chief's kindness, with the chief's justice and wisdom, begat a far warmer esteem for law and order than the most admirable set of rules could ever have inspired.

The difficulties were that the clan system was efficient only within a narrow area; that it gave rise to interminable feuds; and that it was inapplicable to the circumstances created by the rise of modern industry and trade. But may it not be that it was abrogated all too lightly, or at least with too little anxiety to provide for it a proper substitute? At any rate, it realised (in some degree) an ideal which, according to Carlyle, " is the wish and prayer of all human " [political] " hearts, everywhere and at all times " : " give me a leader ; a true leader, not a false, sham leader ; a true leader that he may guide me on the true way, that I may be loyal to him, that I may swear fealty to him, and follow him and feel that it is well with me." And that the political machinery of modern times is adequate to, or suitable for, the attainment of this ideal is as yet by no means clear.

XX.

In Scottish history — ecclesiastical or
political—execution is a less distinctive
feature than assassination. The roll of
the assassinated is probably a more distinguished one than that of the legally
executed, for it embraces several kings
and regents, two Church dignitaries of
the highest rank, and nobles too numerous
to mention. Moreover, assassination acquired in Scotland a certain lustre from
the rank of those who deigned to use it
as a weapon of revenge ; and as practised
under these conditions it far transcends the
rival method in pungency of interest.
Other things being equal, the tragic ele-

ment in assassination greatly exceeds that
associated with the stereotyped legal
methods of terminating life. A peculiar
fascination always attaches to the exhibition of the emotional side of human
nature; and conventionalities being, in
the case of assassination, cast aside, we
have glimpses of character and personality
which could not be otherwise obtained.
Thus Scottish history is necessarily more
edifying to the student of human life
than to the pedantic constitutionalist.
In English history—excepting as regards
the earlier centuries—the position is re-
versed. We have the minute details and
circumstances of several extraordinary plots,
but the catastrophes are, on the whole,
sadly disappointing. True, it will be difficult to find in Scottish annals any piece of
political villainy so pitiful and so base as
the murder of the princes in the Tower;
but this is an exception—literally—that
proves the rule. The very obscurity in
which the crime is shrouded may in itself

be taken to indicate how alien was political
murder to the English habit.

In Scotland assassination was practised
for the most part brazenly and openly; no
special odium appears to have attached to
it; it was a matter rather for boasting than
for shame. But even in the throes of revo-
lution the English nation never lost her
instinctive respect for law and order; and
in the perpetration of her most notorious
political murders she strove at least to
travesty the traditional legal forms. It
follows that for religious or political executions Scotland cannot compare for a
moment to the Southern kingdom. The
martyr-pyres on the Scores at St. Andrew's,
or on the Edinburgh Calton Hill, do pale
their ineffectual fires in the great blaze of
Smithfield; and no spot on Scottish soil
can boast of such a notable assemblage of
the doomed as that which crowds on the
memory at the mention of Tower Hill.
For centuries in Scotland a certain number
of nobles were nearly always at feud with

their sovereign; but they were treated
rather as belligerents than as rebels, and
it was rarely indeed that the extreme
penalty of the law was exercised against
them. Until the Reformation there are
comparatively few deaths of notables at
the instance of government or king; and
some of them—as those of the sixth and
eighth Earls of Douglas—may more fairly
be placed in the category of assassinations.
The case of Sir Robert Graham, however
—the murderer of James I.—stands out
conspicuous for all time by reason of the
almost incredible cruelty of the tortures
(by "hooked instruments of iron all glow-
ing hot") with which he was done to
death. It is a remarkable fact that the
majority of political executions in Scotland, even after the Reformation, were
traceable directly or indirectly to religious
controversy. They date properly from the
construction of the maiden by the Edinburgh magistrates in 1565. It may be
that the need of the maiden was brought

home by the fact that the "auld heiding
sword had failyet," and that the two-
handed sword then bought of William
Macartney was discovered to be inconvenient and unserviceable. Perhaps, too,
so ingenious and consummate an instrument of death was deemed a fitting com-
plement to the more complete judicial
arrangements consequent on the erection of the Tolbooth a few years before.
Anyhow, this same maiden — with the
occasional substitution of a new blade—
continued to figure as the presiding genius
or familiar spirit of the High Street and
the Tolbooth for the next hundred and
fifty years, the scene of her operations
being generally the Cross, but occasionally
the Castle Hill (she appeared in the Grassmarket only once or twice), while the west
gable of the Tolbooth became more and
more hideous with the grisly trophies of
her prowess. Those who caressed were
not necessarily criminals of rank, nor
even political criminals. In Scotland the

ancient custom of reserving the honour of death by decapitation for persons of birth and station had fallen somewhat into desuetude, though strangulation was still regarded as especially opprobrious. Decapitation by the maiden seems, however, to have been chiefly confined to criminals under sentence from the judges of the supreme courts, and for offences of peculiar heinousness—as murder, rape, and treason. None to whom this method of execution was deemed appropriate had been guilty of mere theft; and it must be remembered that while the maiden went on plying at the Cross, the hangman was also at work on the Borough Muir, and afterwards in the Grassmarket. Among the more distinguished of the maiden's victims were the Regent Morton, the Marquis of Argyll, the Earl of Argyll, the Marquis of Huntly and the Earl of Gowrie — all executed at the Cross. Morton had been sentenced to the more shameful death of strangulation, but the sentence was modi-

fied by the king. In two other conspicuous cases—those of the Great Marquis
and Kirkcaldy of Grange—religious bigotry
insured the substitution of strangulation
for decapitation. Both were executed at
the Cross; but the method practised on
the criminals at the Borough Muir was
deemed the more fitting reward of persons
excommunicated by the Kirk. In Montrose's sentence it was specially mentioned
that if at his death he was "penitent and
relaxed from excommunication," the "trunk
of his body" (his limbs were assigned conspicuous positions in the chief towns) was
"to be interred by pioneers in the Grey-
friars, otherwise to be interred in the
Burrow Muir by the hangman's men under
the gallows." The fashion of Kirkcaldy's
death was no doubt determined by what was
held the necessity of fulfilling a prophecy
of good John Knox—that he should "be
brought down over the walls of it" (the
Castle) "with shame, and hung against the
sun"; and, as a fact, he was "put off the

ladder" just after the sun, having passed
the northwest corner of the steeple of St.
Giles, began to gleam down upon the
pitiable scene. "As he was hanging,"
records the devout Calderwood, "his face
was sett towards the east; but within a
prettie space, turned about to the west,
against the sunne, and so remained; at
which time Mr. David" [Lindsay] "marked
him, when all supposed he was dead, to
lift up his hands, which were bound before
him, and to lay them down again softlie;
which moved him with exclamation to
glorify God."

It is a common error to suppose that
Edinburgh has had but two chief places of
execution, the Borough Muir and (later)
the Grassmarket. Even the latest edition
of *Chambers's Encyclopædia* compiled in
this very High Street, within a stone's-
throw of these centres of history, will have
it that "at Edinburgh the place of execution was chiefly in the Grassmarket till
1784, when it was transferred to a plat-

form at the west end of the Tolbooth."
This general forgetfulness of the original
scene of the principal political executions
is a doleful comment on the transiency of
fame. The only political executions of
importance associated with the Grassmarket are those of certain leaders of the
Covenanters—as Johnston of Warriston,
Renwick, and others—all deemed only
worthy of death by strangulation; but in
the case of the Covenanters the extreme
sentence was generally carried into execution immediately after capture, and in
accordance with the regulations of martial
law. The Jacobite risings swelled in no
inconsiderable degree the roll of Scots
political victims; but the trials of the
rebels-in-chief were held in London, and
the Scotsmen who fell under the axe were
made to follow in the footsteps of More and
Cromwell and Strafford and Laud and—
like the Greys, the Dudleys, and the
Howards—they looked their last upon the
world from Tower Hill.

XXI.

THE LOCKMAN.

LOCKMAN, Lokman, or Lockeman is the term — seemingly the soft and delicate adumbration—that Scotsmen were wont to employ to designate the executioner. Everywhere contempt and mockery rather than regard have been his portion; and that a people so accustomed to call a spade not only a spade but something worse should choose him an appellation so apparently colourless and inexpressive might fairly be termed a philological puzzle. Yet the mild signification has been sanctioned—perhaps originated—by Sir Walter himself. "Lockman," thus he has it, "so called from the small quantity of meal"

(Scotticé, " lock ") " which he was entitled
to take out of every boll exposed to market
in the city. In Edinburgh the duty has
been very long commuted ; but in Dumfries
the finisher of the law still exercises, or did
lately exercise, his privilege, the quantity
taken being regulated by a small iron ladle
which he uses in the measurement of his
perquisite." Now the facts on which Sir
Walter's theory rests are indisputable;
indeed, there is an abundance of evidence
that throughout the Land o' Cakes the
"lock" of meal was the hangman's perquisite from time at least anterior to the
period when certain chalders of grain became the legal dues of the parish clergyman.
But this by no means settles the question
how to explain that the hangman's collection of his salary in kind should be
recognised even in his official description—
for lockman was the official as well as the
popular style—as his most distinctive function, all seeming allusion to his specific
duties being omitted. Superficially con-

sidered, the other derivation (originally sanctioned by Jamieson) from the better-known
signification of the word "lock" as part of
a door—the man who locks (*i.e.*, the "dubs-
man or turnkey ")—appears more plausible;
for no doubt the hangman and the gaoler
were pretty often identical, the criminal
being thus under charge of this grim
representative of justice from the time
that in the character of deempster (doom-
ster) he pronounced the sentence of death
against him, until his mortal remains were
finally disposed of. But again there is the
difficulty—how to explain the seemingly
almost morbid tenderness of the Scot's
regard for the hangman's susceptibilities,
in thus dropping all allusion to the more
odious aspects of his office. Be it remembered that the euphimism (if such it were)
was accepted from time immemorial; so that
you read in Blind Harry's "Wallace" that

> "The Lokmen than thei bur Wallace, but baid
> On till a place his martyrdom to tak'."

Indeed, it is by no means improbable

—so far as facts are known—that "lockman" was Scots for "executioner," when
locks in Scotland were not specially associated with security, and sacks of grain
in her market-places were scant and far
between.

But what forbids the supposition that the
epithet sets forth a grim allusion to locks
of another kind? Locks more distinctively
associated with the doomsman's function?
—the locks, to wit, of the man or woman
whose finisher he was? — the locks by
which he grasped the head it was his to
expose to the gaze of the gaping crowd?
Such a derivation, be it observed, is in no
wise made superfluous by the fact that a
"lock," or small handful, of grain, was the
official perquisite; nor does it stand in
contradiction to the custom, nor in the
least diminish its significance. On the
contrary, it would explain (and this in
striking accord with the sordid or brutal
humour from which the Scottish vocabulary derives so much of its vigour) the

origin and signification of the old word
" lock " in Scotland as a quantitative term.
It was the quantity grasped by the executioner : that in any case, whatever else.

But let the derivation of the term be
what it may, the custom referred to is proof
enough that the lockman was very much
in evidence. A superficial observer might
leap to the conclusion that his emoluments
were out of all proportion to his duties.
Surely a handful of grain out of every boll
in the market-place would mean more than
a sufficient supply of food for himself and
his family! And had he not also a livery,
a free house, and a special allowance for
his more important appearances as well?
Plainly, therefore, for an official whose
duties, albeit unenviable, were far from
laborious (much less exhausting), such a
salary would in frugal Scotland have been
deemed inordinate. But in those elder and
sterner years the lockman did by no means
loll away his hours in the listless fashion of
his modern analogue. His life was busy

as well as serious. His diocese, it is true, instead of as now embracing three kingdoms, was contained within the bounds of a single burgh; but in olden time most burghs were able to keep their lockman in constant occupation, while in the larger towns he was fain to delegate some part of his duties to subordinates. For one thing, the death sentence was attached to certain crimes now only visited with imprisonment (as theft and incest), or held deserving of no punishment at all—as adultery or attendance on the mass. Again, the final ceremony was much more complex and more prolonged than now. The criminal was not unaccustomed to address the crowd from the scaffold—occasionally he did so at great length; and when all was over, the body, in the case of strangulation, was commonly suspended for two or three hours before cutting down and decapitating, when it was customary for the hangman to continue his "watch and ward" on the scaffold till the performance of the final rites.

Hence the allusion of Dunbar in his
" Flyting "—

" Ay loungand lyk ane lockman on ane ledder
Thy ghastly luke fleys* folkis that pass the by."

Nor did the lockman's responsibility cease
with the public ceremony, for had he not to
affix the several members of the more noted
victims in conspicuous places, or sometimes
to hang in chains the corse of the heinous
malefactor to dangle and rustle in the wind
till it became a creaking skeleton? And
apart from his deathful duties he had plenty
to do in the way of whipping, branding, and
mutilation. Not only was it his to apply
the severer tortures in cases of exceptional
guilt, whether actual or only suspected; he
had also a well-nigh unbroken round of daily
toil upon the persons of the less heinous.
Many of these were handed over to him for
punishment by the Kirk authorities; and
the Session Records sufficiently indicate how
much his services were in request. Then

* Terrifies.

he was under obligation to carry out the summary sentences of magistrates by bear ing the culprit to the cross and placing him in the jougs ; the application of the pillory —with or without the delicate additions of pinching the nose, nailing the ears, or boring the tongue—usually communicated a spice of daily vivacity to the monotony of burgher life ; the more momentous duty of ducking scolds and adultresses occupied much of his solicitude ; and to have omitted the observance of scourging criminals through the streets would have robbed market days of their primest flavour of felicity. The " hangman's whip " had terrors more immediately effective than the "fear of hell," and perhaps it impressed the popular imagination more powerfully than either block or gallows. In fact, it was chiefly in the lockman that both Church and State reposed their trust for the main- tenance of order and morality. None played so conspicuous a part in the public eye, and none discharged duties deemed more essential to the welfare of society. His present effacement may indicate a marked improvement in morality, or a great advance in civilisation, or the discovery that many of his methods were really mistaken and ineffectual; but it is perhaps the most striking symptom of change to be recorded in the social and ecclesiastical life of Scotland during the last two hundred years.

XXII.

In Scotland the accession of James VI. to the English throne was matter for almost boundless satisfaction. Short of the actual conquest of her "auld enemy," nothing could have touched the nation's vanity to anything like such pleasant purpose. Apparently the problem of the relationship between the two countries had been finally solved, and solved (from a Scottish point of view) in a fashion preposterously felicitous; but it was not long ere the honour done the northern kingdom was discerned to be no more than merely nominal. Except in the rewards bestowed on a few needy courtiers, the real and solid advantages that might

have been expected to follow in its train
were nowhere visible, while the drawbacks of
the new connection were presently a matter
of acute experience. Nominally the era of
avowed hostility was closed, but the new
departure proved as antagonistic to Scottish
national interests as the ancient enmity
itself. The mere transference of the Court
from Edinburgh to London did not involve
a great pecuniary loss; but the attention
of the sovereign was now primarily occupied
with the affairs of the wealthier and more
powerful of his kingdoms, and the prosperity of the other became a matter of less
vital concern to him. By retaining her
legislature Scotland was supposed to retain
her nationality, but it was the shadow without the substance, and the privilege was
attended by evils as great as those of yore,
with none of the old advantages and with
no new ones to atone for their loss. Indeed
there is no more striking fact in Scottish
history than the miserable effect upon Scotland of the simple union of the crowns:

her condition was never more gloomy or
more desperate than during the century or
so that elapsed before the union of the
parliaments.

The existence of a separate legislature
practically nullified many of the good results anticipated from the advent of a Scots
heir to the English throne. As matters
turned out the most distinctive result of
this arrangement was to foster jealousy
between the two countries and to prevent
that fusion of sentiment and interest essential to the common and complete welfare of
both. In other circumstances, and in an
ideal world, it might, could, would, should
have been otherwise; but we are here concerned merely with actual facts, not with
ideal possibilities. For a whole century—
with the exception of eight years—after the
union of the crowns, separate legislatures
existed in Scotland and in England, and the
effect upon the poorer kingdom seems to
have been nothing less than disastrous.
Only once in all the seventeenth century

did she enjoy a flicker of prosperity, and
that was during the eight years of Cromwell's Protectorate, when—her legislative
independence having been snatched from
her by force—she was united to England
on terms of Cromwell's own dictation.
Under the Protectorate Scotland and England were treated in all respects as one,
and immediately the immense advantages
to Scotland began to be manifest. But
Cromwell's rule was too brief to permit of
more than the beginnings of prosperity ;
and at the Restoration she recovered her
old independence, and with it all its previous drawbacks and detriments. By the
English Navigation Act of 1662 she was
debarred from all trade with the English
colonies, and could only use her ships
to bring goods to England not of Scottish
growth or manufacture; she adopted similar
regulations for herself; and trade between
the two countries was further hampered
by enactments made by each in her own
supposed or apparent interests. The

wisdom of these enactments it is un-
necessary to consider; it is enough to note
that they were inevitable while the two
countries remained separate, and that from
their effects it was equally inevitable that
Scotland should be the main if not the only
sufferer. Not only did she fail to keep pace
with the advance of England, but the close
of the century found her even poorer than
at the beginning. "Partly through our
own fault," wrote Fletcher of Saltoun in
1698, "and partly by the removal of our
king into another country, this nation, of
all those who possess good ports and lie
conveniently for trade and fishing, has been
the only part of Europe which did not apply
itself to commerce, and, possessing a barren
country, in less than an age we are sunk to
so low a condition as to be despised by all
our neighbours, and made incapable to repel
an injury if any should be offered." While
England had been laying the foundations
of her great colonial empire, and establish-
ing centres of trade and commerce in well-

nigh every part of the habitable globe, the
foreign trade of Scotland, never of any great
importance, had gradually fallen almost to
zero. Again, the insecurity of the Lowland
districts previous to the union of the crowns
had seriously hindered the growth of towns
and the establishment of manufactures; in
a large proportion of the population there
had been fostered such a habit of rieving
and plundering as made the prosecution
of peaceful industries intolerably irksome,
while the religious conflicts of the century
were strong to distract and divert attention
from commercial enterprise. Theoretically
at least, by some of the sterner fanatics,
the pursuit of riches was held positively
sinful; to the injunction not " to love the
world nor the things of the world " they
pretended to give a rigid and literal interpretation. No doubt also the fines inflicted
upon recusants, and the other hardships
incident to the long period of Covenanting
persecution, had contributed not incon-
siderably to the general impoverishment;

but when, towards the close of the century,
the nation began to turn from barren (certainly in a material, and it is to be feared
also in a spiritual, sense) religious controversy to the promotion of trade and manufactures, some preachers did not fail to
predict that for this preference of temporal
to eternal interests the wrath of the Most
High would sooner or later be made manifest in some signal judgment.

Latterly the nobles themselves were
largely exposed to the stress of indigence.
In ancient times their power and influence
and consequent prosperity depended chiefly
on the numbers of their followers, but with
a greatly increased population and altered
conditions of society this no longer held
good. The poverty which for some generations had preyed upon the general community now began to attack them in turn.
Not only were the majority of them unable
to do anything to promote agricultural or
commercial enterprise, but in London some
of them sank so low as hell-keeping and-

other shifts no whit more reputable. The younger sons of the gentry, finding no sphere for their ambition at home, hired themselves out as mercenaries; but the fortune they won by arms was commonly no greater than that of Rittmaster Dalgetty; and, if at all, it was only negatively that they assisted to relieve the desperate poverty by which their country was prostrated. By the end of the century she had reached a stage of collapse from which unaided it was impossible to rally. Her only manufacture of any particular importance was linen, and its extension was seriously hampered by the English trade restrictions. Other manufactures—as glass, soap, paper, and wool—had been introduced of late, but their progress was preposterously slow. In the conveniences and comforts of civilised life she was miserably behind the rest of Europe. Her commerce with her sister-nations had utterly failed to keep pace with the growth of her population, so that in 1656 her fleet consisted of no more than

137 barques and brigantines, of 5,736 tons
—about a three-hundredth part of her
present tonnage. Scientific agriculture
was yet unknown to her, and for some
centuries her agricultural resources had
remained incapable of expansion. From a
combination of causes she was burdened
with a surplus population over a hundred
thousand strong, who followed no occupation and subsisted upon alms as often
bestowed upon compulsion as from benevo-
lence. She had missed her golden opportunity of colonising and of commerce ; she
had been thrown back upon her barren soil
and her limited acreage ; she had ceased to
possess within herself the means of extri-
cation from the state of grinding poverty to
which she was reduced. Her desperate
circumstances were the more galling in contrast to that magnificent career of adventure
and prosperity upon which her rival had
entered. That in 1696 she should have
embarked with feverish eagerness upon an
enterprise so transparently foolish as the

Darien Expedition can only be explained by the fact that she grasped at this delusive opportunity as her only hope. Rendered desperate by her pitiable plight and by jealousy of England, she staked her whole fortune on this cast of the dice; and the result was such as made union with England inevitable.

If the Darien Expedition had turned out even a partial success, the chances are that the union would have been indefinitely deferred. But even had the scheme been really rational and wise, the country had no sufficient resources within herself to secure its adequate success. To recover herself unaided after so long a period of extreme hardship was practically impossible. Rivalry with England must have severely hampered her commercial enterprise; and the sister kingdom had got such a start in the race that competition was vain. The demonstration of this was the priceless practical lesson enforced by the Darien disaster. The conviction was imposed upon thought-

ful Scotsmen that the achievement of prosperity lay not in the discovering of El
Dorados, but in being admitted to an equal
share in the trading chances of England.
This was the chief inducement to union,
and the Scottish Commissioners demanded
as an essential condition " the mutual communication of trade and other privileges and
advantages." There was a certain naïve
assurance in this way of putting the case:
it was clear to all men that for some time at
least the reciprocity must necessarily be all
on one side, for though England might not
lose—of course she was largely the gainer
—by the proposed arrangement, her new
partner would at least for many years have
much the best of this part of the bargain.
Her hope of profit from trade alliance with
such an insolvent associate must have been
of the slightest, while in Scotland's case the
alliance meant practical salvation. In both
cases the good results far exceeded expectation. England looked for little, and has
profited much; Scotland was reconciled to

the experiment chiefly by ambition to share
in England's prosperity; and the minor
commercial sacrifices made to attain her
purpose were soon discovered to be as
nothing compared with the benefits that
accrued. Hence the lively and lasting
contentment in the union which—after one
or two spasms of jealousy—gradually possessed the Scottish nation: a contentment
scarce broken by so much as a murmur of
regret till recent times. Of course the
prosperity conferred by the union was
somewhat slow in growth. Commercial
vitality had sunk to so low a point that
the development of some symptoms of returning health was of necessity a matter of
years. The earliest indication of a decided
change for the better was the establishment
of the shipping trade of Glasgow and the
Clyde with America and the West Indies.
Its advance was wonderfully rapid, and one
immediate result was the institution of
certain manufactures in several western
villages, which were soon transformed into

populous and thriving towns. This indeed
was the first manifestation of that marvellous
industrial energy which has made Glasgow
and the west one of the great trading centres
of the world. The western capital began to
" flourish " to far better purpose by her
West Indian connection than she had ever
done " through the preaching of the Word "
during the years when visionary Covenanters
" bore the gree " as the ecclesiastical successors of St. Mungo. The effect of the
union on the eastern towns and seaports—
which were much less conveniently placed
for commercial intercourse with the English
colonies and dependencies—was naturally
much less instant and extraordinary. But
throughout Scotland—even in those districts not directly benefited by the establishment of manufactures—the iron grip of
poverty resulting from a surplus population
was soon relaxed. Alike by the attention
they engrossed, the waste of resources they
entailed, and the sense of insecurity they
left behind, the distractions of the '15 and

the '45 were serious hindrances to enterprise ; but after the reduction of the Highlands it was perceived that progress and
prosperity were really paramount all over
the land.

For some time after the union much of
the Scottish trade was carried on in English
vessels, for the simple reason that Scotland
had neither ships of her own nor money
wherewith to build them. The first Scots
trader that crossed the Atlantic was launched
on the Clyde as late as 1718; and forty-two
years after, the national tonnage, which in
1712 is stated to have been only 10,046,
had increased to 53,913, which was more
than trebled before the end of the century.
At the union the linen (the staple manufacture until the introduction of cotton)
made for sale did not exceed 1,500,000
yards ; but in 1727 it was 2,183,978 yards,
in 1735 it was over 4,500,000 yards, in 1760
it was over 10,000,000 yards. Before the
union the Bank of Scotland, founded in
1695, was the only one in the country, and

its existence even was a symptom rather of
national poverty than of national affluence
—its chief business being the lending of
money on heritable bonds. An attempt
to widen the scope and improve the quality
of its operations by the establishment of
branches at Glasgow, Montrose, Dundee,
and Aberdeen turned out a complete failure,
the parent institution soon finding it impossible to maintain them; but after the
union the banking business began gradually
to show unmistakable signs of expansion,
the Royal Bank being established in 1727,
the British Linen Company in 1746, the
Aberdeen Bank in 1749, with two more at
Glasgow in 1749 and 1750. As for agriculture, the union was the signal for the
publication of treatise after treatise upon
husbandry and kindred topics, and for the
foundation (1723) at Edinburgh of the
Society of Improvers; while towards the
latter half of the century many Scots merchants came home from the West Indies
with large fortunes, and, according to Dr.

Somerville, invested these in the purchase of estates, where they further turned their capital to account in stimulating agricultural improvement. Of course it is true that the progress in industrial and commercial enterprise during the years immediately following the union is not to be compared to the extraordinary advance effected by the introduction of machinery towards the end of the century, when, also, was discovered a source of wealth beyond the dreams of avarice in the immense supplies of coal and iron lost until then in Scottish ground. But at the time of the union all that was a century away, and how without the union, and the consequent relief conferred by admittance to equality in trade with England, could Scotland have tided over that century? All things come round to him that can wait; but could Scotland have waited? The attempt it is clear would have entailed an ordeal of hardship and misery almost too terrible to contemplate. This at least she in great part escaped by the union, and it seems equally clear that but for the English connection her industrial effort, even after the introduction of machinery, would have been badly hampered. Indeed it is difficult to understand what stimulus she would have had to mechanical invention while debarred from all trade communication with English colonies and dependencies. Throughout her history she has owed much to the strength of her own right arm, much to the perseverance and hardihood developed by her long struggle with poverty and England. Since the union the richer and stronger nation has also gained in many ways by its partnership with its neighbour's enterprise and skill; but yet in the later accompt between the two the gods have so willed that the balance of benefit is immensely in Scotland's favour.

The Gresham Press,

UNWIN BROTHERS,

CHILWORTH AND LONDON.

Catalogue of Select Books in Belles Lettres,
History, Biography, Theology, Travel,
Miscellaneous, and Books for Children.

Belles Lettres.

Pablo de Ségovie. By Francesco de Quevedo. Illustrated with Sixty Drawings by Daniel Vierge. With an Introduction on Vierge and his Art by Joseph Pennell, and a Critical Essay on Quevedo and his Writings by W. E. Watts. Limited Edition only. Three Guineas nett.

A French Ambassador at the Court of Charles II. (Le Comte de Cominges, 1662-1665). With many Portraits. By J. J. Jusserand. Demy 8vo., cloth gilt.

Jules Bastien Lepage and his Art. A Memoir, by André Theuriet. With which is included Bastien Lepage as Artist, by George Clausen, A.R.W.S.; An Essay on Modern Realism in Painting, by Walter Sickert, N.E.A.C.; and a Study of Marie Bashkirtseff, by Mathilde Blind. Illustrated by Reproductions of Bastien Lepage's Works. Royal 8vo., cloth, gilt tops, 10s. 6d.

The Women of the French Salons. A Series of Articles on the French Salons of the Seventeenth and Eighteenth Centuries. By Amelia G. Mason. Profusely Illustrated. Foolscap folio, cloth, 25s.

These papers treat of the literary, political, and social influence of the women in France, during the two centuries following the foundation of the salons; including pen-portraits of many noted leaders of famous coteries, and giving numerous glimpses of the Society of this brilliant period.

The Real Japan.
Studies of Contemporary Japanese Manners, Morals, Administrations, and Politics. By HENRY NORMAN. Illustrated with about 50 Photographs taken by the Author. Crown 8vo., cloth, 10s. 6d.

EXTRACT FROM PREFACE.—These essays constitute an attempt, *faute de mieux*, to place before the readers of the countries whence Japan is deriving her incentives and her ideas, an account of some of the chief aspects and institutions of Japanese life as it really is to-day.

The Stream of Pleasure.
A Narrative of a Journey on the Thames from Oxford to London. By JOSEPH and ELIZABETH ROBINS PENNELL. Profusely Illustrated by JOSEPH PENNELL. Small Crown 4to., cloth, 7s. 6d.

"Mrs. Pennell is bright and amusing. Mr. Pennell's sketches of river-side bits and nooks are charming ; and a useful practical chapter has been written by Mr. J. G. Legge. The book is an artistic treat."—*Scotsman.*

Gypsy Sorcery and Fortune Telling.
Illustrated by numerous Incantations, Specimens of Medical Magic, Anecdotes and Tales, by CHARLES GODFREY LELAND ("Hans Breitmann"). Illustrations by the Author. Small 4to., cloth, 16s. Limited Edition of 150 Copies, price £1 11s. 6d. nett.

"The student of folk-lore will welcome it as one of the most valuable additions recently made to the literature of popular beliefs."—*Scotsman.*

Esther Pentreath, the Miller's Daughter:
A Cornish Romance. By J. H. PEARCE, Author of "Bernice," &c. 6s.

Mr. LEONARD COURTNEY, M.P., in the *Nineteenth Century* for May, says it is "an idyll that captivates us by its tenderness, its grace, and its beauty. . . . In truth, the special distinction of 'Esther Pentreath' may be said to lie in the poetic gift of its author."

Main - travelled Roads.
Six Mississippi - Valley Stories. By HAMLIN GARLAND. Crown 8vo., cloth, 3s. 6d.

"Main-travelled Roads" depicts the hard life of the average American Farmer and the farm hands. The author has lived the life he tells of, and he may be called a true realist in his art.

The English Novel in the Time of
Shakespeare. By J. J. JUSSERAND, Author of "English Wayfaring Life." Translated by ELIZABETH LEE, Revised and Enlarged by the Author. Illustrated. Demy 8vo., cloth, 21s

"M. Jusserand's fascinating volume."—*Quarterly Review.*

The Fleet : Its River, Prison, and Marriages. By JOHN ASHTON, Author of "Social Life in the Reign of Queen Anne," &c. With 70 Drawings by the Author from Original Pictures. Second and Cheaper Edition, cloth, 7s. 6d.

Romances of Chivalry : Told and Illustrated in Fac-simile by JOHN ASHTON. Forty-six Illustrations. New and Cheaper Edition. Crown 8vo., cloth, 7s. 6d.

"The result (of the reproduction of the wood blocks) is as creditable to his artistic, as the text is to his literary, ability."—*Guardian.*

The Dawn of the Nineteenth Century in
England : A Social Sketch of the Times. By JOHN ASHTON. Cheaper Edition, in one vol. Illustrated. Large crown 8vo., 10s. 6d.

" The book is one continued source of pleasure and interest, and opens up a wide field for speculation and comment, and many of us will look upon it as an important contribution to contemporary history, not easily available to others than close students."—*Antiquary.*

The Temple : Sacred Poems and Private Ejaculations. By Mr. GEORGE HERBERT. New and Fourth Edition, with Introductory Essay by J. HENRY SHORTHOUSE. Small crown, sheep, 5s.

A fac-simile reprint of the Original Edition of 1633.

" This charming reprint has a fresh value added to it by the Introductory Essay of the Author of 'John Inglesant.'"—*Academy.*

Songs, Ballads, and A Garden Play.
By A. MARY F. ROBINSON, Author of "An Italian Garden." With Frontispiece of Dürer's " Melancholia." Small crown 8vo., half bound, vellum, 5s.

" The romantic ballads have grace, movement, passion and strength."—*Spectator.*

" Marked by sweetness of melody and truth of colour "—*Academy*

The Lazy Minstrel. By J. ASHBY-STERRY, Author of " Boudoir Ballads." Fourth and Popular Edition. Frontispiece by E. A. ABBEY. Fcap. 8vo., cloth, 2s. 6d.

" One of the lightest and brightest writers of vers de société."—*St. James's Gazette.*

English Wayfaring Life in the Middle

Ages (XIVth Century). By J. J. JUSSERAND. Translated from the French by LUCY A. TOULMIN SMITH. Illustrated. Fourth Edition. Crown 8vo., cloth, 7s. 6d.

" This is an extremely fascinating book, and it is surprising that several years should have elapsed before it was brought out in an English dress. However, we have lost nothing by waiting."—*Times.*

Dreams.

By OLIVE SCHREINER, Author of " The Story of an African Farm." With Portrait. Third Edition. Fcap. 8vo., buckram, gilt, 6s.

" They can be compared only with the painted allegories of Mr. Watts . . . . The book is like nothing else in English. Probably it will have no successors as it has had no forerunners."—*Athenæum.*

Gottfried Keller :

A Selection of his Tales. Translated, with a Memoir, by KATE FREILIGRATH KROEKER, Translator of " Brentano's Fairy Tales." With Portrait. Crown 8vo., cloth, 6s.

" The English reader could not have a more representative collection of Keller's admirable stories."—*Saturday Review.*

The Trials of a Country Parson :

Some Fugitive Papers by Rev. A. JESSOPP, D.D., Author of " Arcady," "'The Coming of the Friars," &c. Crown 8vo., cloth, 7s. 6d.

"Sparkles with fresh and unforced humour, and abounds in genial common-sense."—*Scotsman.*

The Coming of the Friars,

And other Mediæval Sketches. By the Rev. AUGUSTUS JESSOPP, D.D., Author of " Arcady : For Better, For Worse," &c. Third Edition. Crown 8vo., cloth, 7s. 6d.

" Always interesting and frequently fascinating."—*St. James's Gazette.*

Arcady :

For Better, For Worse. By AUGUSTUS JESSOPP, D.D., Author of " One Generation of a Norfolk House." Portrait. Popular Edition. Crown 8vo., cloth, 3s. 6d.

" A volume which is, to our minds, one of the most delightful ever published in English."—*Spectator.*

Robert Browning : Personal Notes.

Frontispiece. Small crown 8vo., parchment, 4s. 6d.

" Every lover of Browning will wish to possess this exquisitely-printed and as exquisitely-bound little volume."—*Yorkshire Daily Post.*

Old Chelsea. A Summer-Day's Stroll. By Dr. Benjamin Ellis Martin. Illustrated by Joseph Pennell. Third and Cheaper Edition. Square imperial 16mo., cloth, 3s. 6d.

"Dr. Martin has produced an interesting account of old Chelsea, and he has been well seconded by his coadjutor."—*Athenæum.*

Euphorion : Studies of the Antique and the Mediæval in the Renaissance. By Vernon Lee. Cheap Edition, in one volume. Demy 8vo., cloth, 7s. 6d.

"It is the fruit, as every page testifies, of singularly wide reading and independent thought, and the style combines with much picturesqueness a certain largeness of volume, that reminds us more of our earlier writers than those of our own time."
Contemporary Review.

Studies of the Eighteenth Century in Italy. By Vernon Lee. Demy 8vo., cloth, 7s. 6d.

"These studies show a wide range of knowledge of the subject, precise investigation, abundant power of illustration, and hearty enthusiasm. . . . The style of writing is cultivated, neatly adjusted, and markedly clever."—*Saturday Review.*

Belcaro : Being Essays on Sundry Æsthetical Questions. By Vernon Lee. Crown 8vo., cloth, 5s.

Juvenilia : A Second Series of Essays on Sundry Æsthetical Questions. By Vernon Lee. Two vols. Small crown 8vo., cloth, 12s.

"To discuss it properly would require more space than a single number of 'The Academy' could afford."—*Academy.*

Baldwin : Dialogues on Views and Aspirations. By Vernon Lee. Demy 8vo., cloth, 12s.

"The dialogues are written with . . . an intellectual courage which shrinks from no logical conclusion."—*Scotsman.*

Ottilie : An Eighteenth Century Idyl. By Vernon Lee. Square 8vo., cloth extra, 3s. 6d.

"A graceful little sketch. . . . Drawn with full insight into the period described."—*Spectator.*

Introductory Studies in Greek Art. Delivered in the British Museum by Jane E. Harrison. With Illustrations. Second Edition. Square imperial 16mo., 7s. 6d.

"The best work of its kind in English."—*Oxford Magazine.*

The Wider Hope : Essays and Strictures on the Doctrine and Literature of a Future. By Numerous Writers, Lay and Clerical : Canon FARRAR, the late Principal TULLOCH, the late Rev. J. BALDWIN BROWN, and many others. Crown 8vo., cloth, 7s. 6d.

"A mass of material which will certainly prove useful to students of the subject. Here they will find a large body of valuable opinion on a topic perennially attractive."—*Globe.*

" Expositions." By the Rev. SAMUEL COX, D.D. In Four Vols., demy 8vo., cloth, price 7s. 6d. each.

"We have said enough to show our high opinion of Dr. Cox's volume. It is indeed full of suggestion. . . . A valuable volume."—*The Spectator.*

"Here, too, we have the clear exegetical insight, the lucid expository style, the chastened but effective eloquence, the high ethical standpoint, which secured for the earlier series a well-nigh unanimous award of commendation."—*Academy.*

"When we say that the volume possesses all the intellectual, moral, and spiritual characteristics which have won for its author so distinguished a place among the religious teachers of our time . . . what further recommendation can be necessary ?"—*Nonconformist.*

Inspiration and the Bible : An Inquiry. By ROBERT HORTON, M.A., formerly Fellow of New College, Oxford. Fourth and Cheaper Edition. Crown 8vo., cloth, 3s. 6d.

"The work displays much earnest thought, and a sincere belief in, and love of the Bible."—*Morning Post.*

"It will be found to be a good summary, written in no iconoclastic spirit, but with perfect candour and fairness, of some of the more important results of recent Biblical criticism."—*Scotsman.*

Faint, yet Pursuing. By the Rev. E. J. HARDY, Author of " How to be Happy though Married." Sq. imp. 16mo., cloth, 6s. Cheaper Edition, 3s. 6d.

"One of the most practical and readable volumes of sermons ever published. They must have been eminently hearable."—*British Weekly.*

The Ethic of Freethought : A Selection of Essays and Lectures. By KARL PEARSON, M.A., formerly Fellow of King's College, Cambridge. Demy 8vo., cloth, 12s.

"Are characterised by much learning, much keen and forcible thinking, and a fearlessness of denunciation and exposition."—*Scotsman.*

Climbers' Guide to the Central Pennine.
By WILLIAM MARTIN CONWAY. 32mo., limp cloth, with pocket, flap, and pencil, 10s.

Courts and Sovereigns of Europe.
By "POLITIKOS." Being Full Descriptions of the Home and Court life of the Reigning Families. With many Portraits. Crown 8vo., cloth, 10s. 6d.

"A most interesting and useful volume. . . . . Lively and very readable chapters."—*Pall Mall Gazette.*

The Folks o' Carglen.
A Story. By ALEXANDER GORDON, Author of "What Cheer, O?" Crown 8vo., buckram, 6s.

"A series of sketches, slight in character, but admirably true to nature. . . . Bright and interesting."—*Scotsman.*

Hanging in Chains.
By ALBERT HARTSHORNE, F.S.A. With Eight Illustrations. Demy 12mo., parchment boards, gilt tops, 4s. 6d.

"Mr. Hartshorne illustrates his text by many curious and instructive plates, which form a specially interesting feature. He has done his work very thoroughly, and his book will be found not only very readable, but worthy of preservation."
Globe.

A Vindication of the Rights of Woman:
With Strictures on Political and other Subjects. By MARY WOLLSTONECRAFT. New Edition. With Introduction by Mrs. HENRY FAWCETT. Crown 8vo., cloth, 7s. 6d.

"Mrs. Fawcett's introduction is an admirable and perfectly dispassionate analysis of the main arguments of the book."—*Manchester Guardian.*

Emigration and Immigration:
A Study in Social Science.
By RICHMOND M. SMITH, Professor of Political Economy and Social Science in Columbia College. Square imp. 16mo., cloth, 7s. 6d.

Prof. Smith's book is a popular examination of one of the most urgent of present-day problems from historical, statistical, and economic points of view, the information being full and exact, and the author's style being a model of terseness and clearness.

978-3-74472-992-5

Old-World Scotland - Glimpses of its Modes and Manners is an unchanged, high-quality reprint of the original edition of 1893.
Hansebooks is editor of the literature on different topic areas such as research and science, travel and expeditions, cooking and nutrition, medicine, and other genres. As a publisher we focus on the preservation of historical literature. Many works of historical writers and scientists are available today as antiques only. Hansebooks newly publishes these books and contributes to the preservation of literature which has become rare and historical knowledge for the future.

ISBN/EAN: 978-3-74472-992-5
www.hansebooks.com

hanse